SEW Illustrated

35 Charming Fabric & Thread Designs

16 Zakka Projects

Minki Kim and Kristin Esser

stashBOOKS®

an imprint of C&T Publishing

Publisher: Amy Marson

Creative Director: Gailen Runge

Editor: Lynn Koolish

Technical Editors: Alison M. Schmidt and Debbie Rodgers

Cover/Book Designer: Page + Pixel

Production Coordinator: Zinnia Heinzmann

Production Editors: Jessie Brotman and Alice Mace Nakanishi

Illustrators: Minki Kim and Zinnia Heinzmann

Photo Assistant: Carly Jean Marin

Style photography by Page + Pixel and instructional photography by Diane Pedersen, unless otherwise noted

Published by Stash Books, an imprint of C&T Publishing, Inc., P.O. Box 1456, Lafayette, CA 94549

Library of Congress Cataloging-in-Publication Data

Names: Kim, Minki, 1973- author. | Esser, Kristin, 1966- author.

Title: Sew illustrated : 35 charming fabric & thread designs : 16 zakka projects / Minki Kim and Kristin Esser.

Description: Lafayette, CA : Stash Books, an imprint of C&T Publishing, Inc., [2016]

Identifiers: LCCN 2016000614 | ISBN 9781617451782 (soft cover)

Subjects: LCSH: Sewing. | House furnishings: | Notions (Merchandise)

Classification: LCC TT715 .K555 2016 | DDC 646--dc23

LC record available at https://lccn.loc.gov/2016000614

Printed in China

10 9 8 7 6 5 4 3 2 1

DEDICATION

From Minki:

To my husband, Alex. Thank you for being the same man I met 13 years ago. And my three C's—Caylin, Chloe, and Claire. You always make me want to be a better person.

From Kristin:

For Mom, who instilled in me a love of sewing. I miss you every day. And for my family—Gary, Chloe, Jonah, and Ben. You are my world.

ACKNOWLEDGMENTS

Writing this book was a dream come true, and there are so many people to thank who made it possible.

First of all, thank you to the wonderful people at C&T Publishing for believing in the idea and helping to make this dream a reality, especially Roxane and Lynn. You were a pleasure to work with.

We owe a debt of gratitude to our pattern testers, Jonal Beck, Philipa Core (Ozzypip), Pamela Edwards, Kristi Ryan, and Vicki Tymczyszyn. Thank you for spending your personal time to make this a better book.

Thank you to the companies that supported us with materials to create these projects: Aurifil, buttons.com, C&T Publishing, DMC, The Fat Quarter Shop, Greyline Linens, Jillibean Soup, Just Another Button Company, Penny Rose Fabrics, Riley Blake Fabrics, Sew Me A Song, Simplicity, United Notions/Moda, Vintage Notion, and The Warm Company. Your materials are a joy to work with and we couldn't have done it without you!

CONTENTS

Introduction

A NOTE FROM MINKI

Sewing illustration is my passion, and I could not be more excited to share it with you. I am often asked how the technique is done, and I am so happy to have a whole book explaining it in detail to share with you. My journey to sewing illustration has been a gradual one: I moved to the United States from Korea shortly after getting married, and not knowing anyone here, I began looking for a way to fill the hours. I soon turned to hand sewing, embroidery, and creating handmade dolls as a creative outlet.

One day, my husband brought home a sewing machine, and I found a corner in our tiny apartment to tuck it into. At this point, I had been hand embroidering my drawings and wondered if I could do the same thing with the sewing machine. With some practice, I found that not only could I recreate my drawings on the sewing machine, but it was much faster and I could create even more detailed designs. Soon, I began adding bits of fabric to add interest to my creations, and sewing illustration was born. To this day, I think of sewing illustration as simply drawing with thread.

In the beginning, much of my inspiration came from photos that I took with my phone when I was out on a walk or at the park with my girls. When I returned home, I would head to my sewing area and recreate these images with

my sewing machine. About this time I began my Korean blog (blog.naver.com/zeriano) and started creating a new project nearly every day to share with my readers. I soon found that sewing illustration could be used to embellish any type of project, from coasters to zipper pouches to works of art for the living room wall. I eventually started an English blog (minkikim.com) and also began sharing my creations on Instagram. I love these creative outlets and the inspiration and encouragement I get from being a part of the online sewing community.

Perhaps the most important thing that I hope you take away from this book is the importance of taking time to be creative every day. I truly feel that sewing has changed my life and changed how I look at my life. It is so easy to get lost in the busyness of keeping a home and raising children. But I have found that taking time to sew, even if just for a few stolen moments here and there—at the park, at the pool, or at my sewing machine—provides me with the energy to tackle the rest of my day with a smile.

I hope this technique of drawing with thread will open a new door of creativity for you. It has enriched my life in so many ways and I am so happy to share it with you.

—*Minki*

A NOTE FROM KRISTIN

Sewing has been a part of my life for as long as I can remember. My mother made my clothes when I was a toddler, stitched every Halloween costume with love, and even designed and sewed the drapes for our home. As a teenager, I continued this tradition and made clothes, and as a young adult fresh out of college, I happily began sewing for my new apartment. I stitched up all manner of puffy valances, throw pillows, and toaster covers. After I got married and had a family, my interests turned to quilting and creating items for my home. I delighted in seeing my children snuggled on the sofa with a quilt that I had made, bread rising under a hand-embroidered tea towel, and a hand-knit dishcloth in the sink.

One day, when walking my son to school, I noticed that a new family had moved in down the street and there was a sewing machine right there in the window. I decided then and there to befriend this new neighbor. Up until this point I had no real-life sewing or crafting friends. Thanks to the Internet, I was inspired on a daily basis, but I had no one to chat with about this passion. That sewing machine in the window was Minki's, and we became fast friends over many cups of coffee and tea. I was completely amazed when she shared her work with me. I knew then that the sewing community needed to see her work, and we began making plans for this book. It has been my pleasure to help create this book so that you too can make these lovely projects embellished with sewing illustration.

Minki amazes me with her drawings all the time. When we started this book, I was not confident in my drawing skills. However, using the techniques in this book, I have seen my skills improve with each project. You don't have to be able to draw to create these lovely designs. But if you can, you can take what you learn here and use it as a jumping-off point for your own one-of-a-kind creations. My message to you is to enjoy the process, explore this new technique, and embrace taking time out of your day to sew and nurture your creativity.

—*Kristin*

I think of sewing illustration as simply drawing with thread. —MINKI

Basic Techniques

Sewing illustration is a fun and versatile technique that you can use to enhance and embellish many types of sewing projects. One of the best things about this technique is that it can be as simple or elaborate as you like. Start with simple designs and projects and watch your skills grow as you work your way through the projects in this book. Then apply the technique to your own projects. The options are endless!

Read through this chapter carefully to understand the basics; then experiment to find the techniques that work best for you.

TIP *There are many ways to transfer designs and create fabric accents; you will see these used throughout the book. Try different techniques to find the ones that work best for you.*

TRANSFERRING A DESIGN TO FABRIC

The first step in sewing illustration is to transfer a design onto fabric. There are many ways to transfer the designs and motifs provided in this book onto your fabric. Some work better than others, and sometimes the choice is just a matter of personal preference. None of them require a big investment, so you may want to pick up the materials for a few different techniques and experiment to find out what you like best.

IRON-ON TRANSFERS

All the sewing illustration designs are provided as iron-on transfers (pullout pages P1 and P2). These transfers can be used multiple times, but the ink will appear lighter with each use. The ink may fade with time but does not wash out, so make sure to cover the lines with stitching.

1. Cut out the desired design.

2. Heat the iron up to the hottest setting. Preheat the fabric by ironing it before you place your design on it.

3. Place the design ink-side down on the right side of the fabric. Press for 12–15 seconds. Do not glide the iron back and forth, as that may smear the ink. The marks will appear darker the longer you iron.

4. To check if the design has transferred, carefully lift up one corner of the paper, without shifting the design. If it is not dark enough, press for a few more seconds.

WINDOW/LIGHTBOX METHOD

One of the simplest methods is to make a photocopy of the design and tape it to a bright window.

1. Place a piece of linen (or your preferred background fabric) over the design and tape it in place, positioning the design in the correct location. Of course, if you have a lightbox, tracing is even easier, but a lightbox isn't necessary.

2. After the linen and design are secure, trace the design with a temporary marking pen. My favorite is the Frixion erasable pen by Pilot. It comes in many colors, but we suggest using black. This pen makes a clean, thin line that disappears when you run an iron over the marks. Remember that this ink is temperature sensitive, so storing your marked fabric in a very hot environment, like a car on a sunny day, may cause the marks to disappear. Freezing temperatures will bring the marks back. Another choice is a water-soluble marker. Use one with a fine tip, since the ink spreads a bit on the fabric, creating a thicker line. After sewing, you can remove the marks with a bit of cold water. *Make sure you don't iron over the marks or they may become permanent!*

WASH-AWAY STABILIZER

This may be one of the easiest methods of transfer. A wash-away stabilizer product, such as Wash-Away Stitch Stabilizer (by C&T Publishing), has a rough side and a sticky backing, covered with paper. Always read the manufacturer's instructions first and test how to best copy or print on the stabilizer. Photocopiers or printers that use heat (that is, toner-based machines) *cannot* be used.

1. Scan and print or copy the motifs on the wash-away stabilizer using an inkjet printer, or trace the motif directly onto the rough side. It is very easy because the stabilizer is quite transparent. You can use any type of marking device—pencil, pen, anything.

2. Peel the paper away from the backing and stick it onto the fabric.

3. Sew right on top of the stabilizer. The outlines are very clear with this method, making them easy to follow. When the design is complete, rinse the fabric with cool water under the faucet to remove the stabilizer.

The only downside to this method is that you are left with a wet piece of fabric, but you may be able to dry it quickly with an iron. Or, just move on to the construction of a different part of your project while it dries.

TRACING/TRANSFER PAPER

There are several types of tracing/transfer paper available, both wax-based and wax-free (usually chalk-based). We don't recommend the wax-free type, because we have never been able to get a dark enough mark with that method. The wax-based paper, such as Simplicity Dressmaker's Tracing Paper, does a better job, but the marks can be quite light.

1. Make a copy of the motif you would like to transfer. Cut it out leaving about a ½" border around the motif.

2. On a hard surface, such as a table or cutting mat, place the printout on the linen in the desired location. Once you have it in the correct place, slip a piece of tracing paper between the paper and the fabric. Make sure that the wax side is touching the fabric.

3. Using a sharp pencil, trace the design, using hard pressure. Check how well your first lines show up before tracing the entire design. You may want to trace over it a couple of times, just to be sure that it has transferred.

4. After you are done sewing over this design, you can remove the marks by applying some cold water. I have found that sometimes a few faint marks might remain, so use this method with caution and really try to cover the marks when stitching over them.

HEAT TRANSFER PENCIL

1. Make a copy of the design you want to use. To prevent your design from being reversed, flip over the paper and outline the design with the heat transfer pencil on the back of the paper. Press hard to get a good, solid mark, but try not to make the lines too thick.

2. Cut out the design and iron it onto the linen in the desired spot, following the manufacturer's instructions.

The upside of this method is that it is easier to trace the design on paper than on fabric, but the downside is that the marks can be a little thick, and they are not removable. So it is important that you completely cover the marks with your stitching.

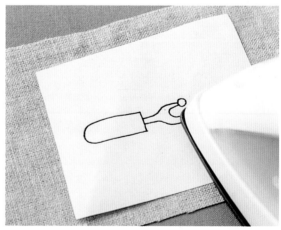

TABLET/SMARTPHONE

You can actually use a tablet or smartphone as a small lightbox.

1. Take a picture of the pattern in the book and bring it up in a photo app. One benefit of this method is that you can easily resize the image right on the screen of the device.

2. When you have the size you want, place the fabric over the screen and trace.

WARNING: *Make sure you have a screen protector on your device so that you don't scratch the screen!*

RUBBER STAMP

Though not currently available for any of the designs in this book, another method of transferring a motif onto fabric is a rubber stamp. Test scrapbooking and fabric inks to find one that won't bleed if it gets wet, and follow any manufacturer's instructions regarding heat setting.

1. Choose a stamp with an image that you like, but stay away from ones that have a lot of detail that will be hard to stitch. Simple designs work best.

2. Ink the stamp and lightly stamp the linen.

The ink will be permanent, so you will need to make sure that you stamp carefully and completely cover the marks with stitching.

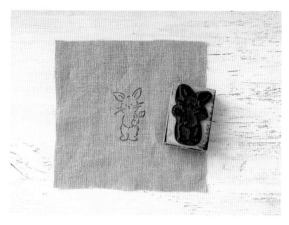

JUST DRAW!

Lastly, you can just draw right on the fabric. A Frixion pen is the perfect tool for this. If you are confident in your drawing skills, then use the designs in this book as inspiration for your own personal works of art (or make up your own designs). It takes a bit of practice to draw on linen, as it is quite stretchy—iron some light- or midweight fusible interfacing on the wrong side of the linen to stabilize the fabric in preparation for drawing. Take your time, practice, and let your own creativity shine through!

SEWING ILLUSTRATION

PREPARING THE FABRIC FOR SEWING

After you have transferred the design to the linen, you need to stabilize the fabric while you are sewing. There are a few ways to do this, depending on the project.

- **Embroidery Backing Paper or Stabilizer:** Cut out a piece of backing paper or stabilizer a little bigger than your design and place it under the linen before you start to sew. You can pin it in place if you wish or just place it where you need it. Your beginning stitches will hold it in place once you start to sew.

- **Batting:** If your project has batting in it, as do the coasters and tea mats, you can use the batting as a stabilizer. We suggest 100% cotton quilt batting, but use what you prefer. You can either use fusible batting, fusing it to the wrong side of the linen, or simply put the linen on top of the batting and start stitching. Pin in place if desired.

THREAD

Note: *The larger the thread-weight number, the finer the thread—for example, a 40-weight thread is thinner than a 12-weight.*

For the sewing illustration to really stand out, use a heavier-weight thread than what you use to construct the projects; 40-weight thread works well, as does 12-weight thread from Aurifil (one of Minki's favorites). However, if you don't have any heavier-weight thread, go ahead and try it with whatever thread you happen to have (usually 50-weight). You may just have to sew around the outline of your design an extra time or two to get the thickness you want. Dark brown thread was used in almost all projects.

You can use the same thread or a lighter-weight thread in the bobbin. The bobbin thread doesn't have to be heavier; standard 50-weight thread is fine.

DRAWING WITH THREAD

Sewing illustration is simply drawing with thread. Just as you might use a pen with a thicker or thinner tip to create the look you want when drawing, play around with different weights of thread in the same way. Sometimes you'll want a heavier outline, almost like a hand-embroidered look, and can use an 8- or 12-weight thread. But sometimes a more delicate line is what a design calls for, so try 40- or 50-weight thread. There are times when you might need to outline a design several times to achieve the look you want, and sometimes once will be sufficient. Play around to find the look and thread weights that you prefer.

STITCH LENGTH

You can do sewing illustration on any type of sewing machine; no special equipment is required. The first thing you need to do is to shorten the stitch length. Check the user's manual if you don't know how to change the stitch length. For a look similar to the projects presented in this book, set it somewhere between 1.4 and 1.8. There are a few reasons for shortening the stitch length. The first is that the smaller the stitch is, the smoother the line of stitching is, which creates a look that resembles drawing. If your design is large and simple, a 1.8 will work fine, but if it is smaller and more detailed, especially if it has curves, you will get a smoother line from a stitch length of 1.6 or 1.4. Smaller stitch lengths do slow down the sewing, so you have to find the balance that works for you.

SEWING MACHINE FEET

- **Open-toe appliqué foot:** An open-toe appliqué foot, especially a clear plastic one, provides maximum visibility when stitching sewing illustration. If your sewing machine did not come with one, you may find it a good investment.

- **Standard presser foot:** For many years, Minki used a standard sewing machine foot, so if you don't have an appliqué foot, don't let that stop you. Depending on the type of sewing machine you have, these feet can vary. Some are clear plastic, which will help you see your design while you are sewing. However, even if yours is not completely clear plastic you may find that it works just fine.

- **Darning foot:** If you are a free-motion quilter, you may be very comfortable using a darning foot to do your sewing illustration. If that works for you, by all means do it! If you use a darning foot, you won't have to worry about setting the stitch length, as you control that yourself. Just make sure that your stitches are small enough to achieve a smooth line, especially on curves and smaller details.

Open-toe appliqué feet

Standard presser feet

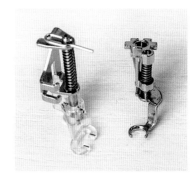

Darning feet

Go slowly. You may even want to slow down the speed of your sewing machine, if it has that capability. As you sew, look ahead a little bit to see where the outline is going. When you get to a curve, slow down and turn the fabric every couple of stitches as you go slowly around the curve. Try keeping one finger on the presser foot lever as you sew around curves, so that it is easy to pick up the presser foot and turn the work a little bit with each stitch, for a nice, smooth curve. If you have a sewing machine with a knee lift, this is even easier.

After you have transferred your design onto the linen, stabilized the fabric, chosen your thread, and set your stitch length, you are ready to begin! But where do you start? To minimize the stops and starts when sewing, look at the design and try to find a place to start where you can create a long line of stitching.

After you have found your starting point, line up your needle on the outline of the design and start sewing.

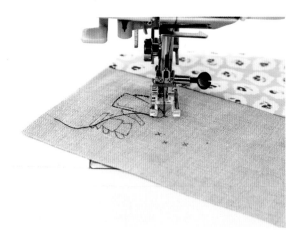

Remember, the drawing is just a guide. Don't be afraid to deviate from the drawing a bit if you are using a temporary marking pen.

After outlining the design the first time, take your project out of the sewing machine and look at it. Look for any little imperfections that you don't like; if you outline it a second time you can correct those little areas. You can sew a smoother curve on a cup handle and never even see that it was a little off at first. You can thicken up an area with a shadow that was not quite right the first time. Each outline gives the project depth and charm. Congratulations! You are now drawing with thread!

This is an example of one of Minki's earlier pieces. She says: "My technique has improved with daily practice, but I love this piece just as much as the work I do now."

TIP *Let go of perfectionism! Each project is a unique work of art. It doesn't have to be perfect to be beautiful! Enjoy the process, practice, and it will get easier. It is often the imperfections that create the charm.*

When stitching around a design for sewing illustration, instead of locking your stitches by sewing back and forth at the beginning and end, simply sew around the design and overlap your stitching about ¼˝. The stitching will be secure.

Many of the projects in this book combine sewing illustration with fabric accents. This technique is very similar to the basic sewing illustration technique, with just a few added steps.

CREATING FABRIC ACCENTS

After you transfer your design onto the fabric, cut out small pieces of fabric to add charm and character to your design. There are a few ways to do this.

Wash-Away Stabilizer

Wash-away stabilizer also works well with fabric accents.

1. Scan or copy the motif and print using an inkjet printer or trace the motif directly onto the rough side of the wash-away stabilizer (see Wash-Away Stabilizer, page 7). Do not use a laser printer or it will melt the stabilizer (not good for the laser printer, either).

2. Cut out each area of the design that you want to use a fabric accent for. Peel the paper away from the backing and stick it right onto the fabric. Trim away the excess fabric.

3. Glue the fabric accent to the desired place on the background fabric.

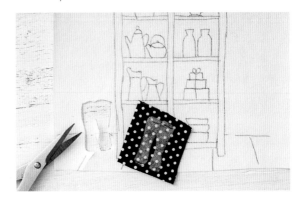

Paper-Backed Fusible Web

The advantage of using fusible web, such as Steam-A-Seam, is that you don't need to secure the fabric accents by stitching them down; you can skip straight to outlining. You may also find that you don't need to use embroidery backing paper or stabilizer with this method.

1. Trace or print the design directly on the paper side of the fusible web. **Be sure to reverse the design.**

2. Roughly cut out each piece and stick or lightly fuse it onto the **wrong side** of the fabric.

3. Cut out the fabric shape on the traced line. Remove the paper backing.

4. Place the shape on the background fabric in the desired location and iron to fuse permanently.

Freezer Paper

Using freezer paper is an easy way to get very accurate designs.

1. Make templates by tracing the desired shapes onto the paper side (the side that is not shiny) of the freezer paper.

2. Cut the shapes out, leaving at least a ¼″ border of paper around each shape.

3. Iron these templates onto the right side of the desired fabric (shiny side down).

4. Cut out the shapes along the traced lines.

Tracing

This is the method to try if you don't have any freezer paper.

1. Make a copy of the design on plain paper and cut it out.

2. Place this cut-out template on the fabric and trace around it with a temporary marking pen, such as a Frixion pen or water-soluble marker.

Depending on the size of the motif, you may want to pin the template down.

Eyeball It

With this method, just look at the shape of the area that needs an accent and cut it out freehand with small scissors. Try it! You will get better at it with time, and the imperfect look is charming.

TIP *Don't worry about small "mistakes." It's okay to leave them or camouflage them with more outlining. If you just can't live with the mistake, go ahead and take the time to rip it out and try again.*

PUTTING IT TOGETHER

Now that you have transferred your design onto the fabric and cut out the fabric accents, it's time to put the motif together. Start with the fabric accents and then do some sewing illustration to add details and depth.

Attaching Fabric Accents

Peel off any backing or freezer paper from the accent pieces. Using a bit of glue, attach each fabric accent in the proper place. If you are using fusible web or wash-away stabilizer, iron the accents onto the background fabric. If you have items stacked on top of each other, like a teacup on top of a saucer, make sure you place the background elements first (glue down the saucer first and then the teacup on top).

Redraw any necessary stitching lines on top of the fabric accents.

TIP *You can use a specialized fabric glue stick, such as one made by Sewline or Roxanne Glue-Baste-It, but a children's washable school glue stick works just fine.*

Securing Pieces

At this point, it's a good idea to secure each piece with a neutral-color thread. You want to be sure that the pieces will not come off when the project is laundered. Stitch about ⅛″ inside the edge of each shape. For larger pieces, such as teapots or tablecloths, stitch a small crosshatch or meander design across each piece. This secures the fabric and adds a bit of depth to the design.

If you have used fusible web you can skip this step, since the fabric accents are already fused to the background fabric.

Stitching

Now that the fabric accents are secured, it's time to develop the details of your design. Start with the largest element in the design and work from there. Find a spot on the design where you can begin outlining that will create a nice, long line. Plan out your design, minimizing starts and stops for a cleaner look.

Set your stitch length to somewhere between 1.4 and 1.8, depending on how small and curvy the shape is. A smaller stitch length will give better results on a smaller or curvier piece. Stitch around the outline of the fabric accent, just inside the raw edge of the fabric. Add sewing illustration details according to your design to add complexity and interest to your project. Refer to Thread-Only Designs (page 12) for additional details on drawing with thread.

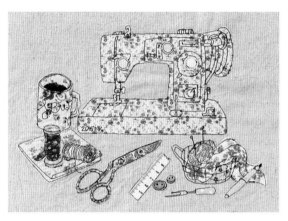

Many projects call for finishing up with hand sewing. Use whatever kind of needle you feel most comfortable with. In general, use a thin needle that still has an eye large enough that you don't struggle to thread it—find what works for you.

TIP *Keep your practice designs and use them to embellish other sewing projects. You can sew them onto coasters and bags, and even patch your children's jeans with them. Don't let them go to waste!*

Any of the designs in this book can be created with hand embroidery if you prefer—the results are equally charming. With machine sewing, you can create things faster and you may find that you can get a level of detail that you can't get with hand embroidery. Hand embroidery using a standard embroidery needle is a lovely embellishment around the edges of many projects.

When sewing by hand, be sure to bury the knots so they don't show on the back. Take a stitch from the front of the linen, with the needle coming up where you want your first stitch to start. Give your thread a little tug until the knot pops under the fabric. Begin the running stitch. At the end of your stitching, tie a small knot in the thread about ¼" from the fabric. Take a small stitch, tug the knot under the fabric, and clip the thread.

STRAIGHT STITCHING If you have a hard time keeping your running stitches straight when stitching lines, use a ruler and an erasable pen such as a Frixion or water-soluble marking pen to draw guidelines. Remove the lines when you are done.

DESIGN TIPS FROM MINKI

I trained as an artist when I was younger, and when I got married and became a mother I wondered if all that training had gone to waste. I realize now that I use the basic design concepts I learned then in all my projects now. I want to pass on to you a few of these basic principles so that you can take what you have learned in this book and create your own designs and projects with confidence. I find that these principles are useful not only in sewing but also in areas such as decorating my home and even fashion.

80/20 RULE

Every time I begin to design a project, I start with linen. I think of linen as blank canvas on which I can bring my designs to life. In fact, I think of sewing illustration as just another method of drawing. One of the simplest rules that I apply to almost every project is the 80/20 Rule. I prefer 80 percent neutral fabric, usually linen, and 20 percent for the design or area with more color. This neutral palette with just the right amount of bright color or motif draws the eye to the design without distraction.

This dessert mat illustrates the use of a large area of neutral fabric with a pop of color for the design.

RULE OF THIRDS

I also look at the project as a whole to decide where I want to put the design. I rarely center motifs, preferring to apply the Rule of Thirds. I find it much more pleasing for most designs to be placed in the lower third of a project or at the intersection of two lines, using the Rule of Thirds. These are not hard-and-fast rules, but they are very handy to think about when deciding where to place your design.

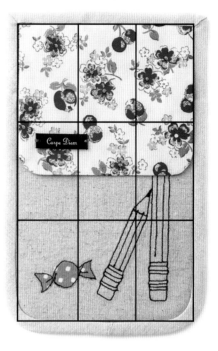

This pencil case illustrates the Rule of Thirds, with the design placed in the lower and right thirds of the project rather than centered.

FABRIC SELECTION

I love picking out the fabrics for my projects. In fact, I think I spend more time deciding on fabric choices than I actually spend sewing. I understand that not everyone feels this way, so let me provide a few guiding principles for you.

- Use fabric that you love. I happen to love bright fabrics, especially yellows and reds. I tend toward 1930s reproduction fabrics, as I find them charming and they work well with linen. Because I like brighter colors, I make sure that all the colors that I use in a project harmonize. If I am using brights, then I use all brights. For example, if I am using a fabric with bright red cherries, then

I don't want to use a duller red somewhere else in the project. The two reds just don't harmonize well. However, if you are partial to more muted tones, then a bright red would probably look out of place, so stick with all muted tones.

- I find inspiration for color combinations all over the place. Just take a look at your children's clothing, interior decor items, and even cereal boxes! Professional designers create these products, and you can learn from the choices they make. Experiment with combinations that appeal to you.

- Think about what area of the design you want to stand out. Choose brighter colors for those elements. The eye is drawn to the highest-contrast area, so make sure that it is the most important part of your design.

I like to make sure that all my fabrics harmonize well together. When using brights, use all brights.

EMBELLISHMENTS

I find that embellishing my projects is one of my favorite parts of the process. I love adding small pops of color with little buttons and tags and hand-embroidered details. I think that taking the time to include these little details adds immeasurably to the charm of the project. So even if you are new to embellishing, I encourage you to slow down and enjoy the final stages of the projects in this book. You may find that you have a passion for embellishment as well.

Embellishments add so much charm to projects—I feel they complete the story. Don't skip this part!

Interfacing

Many of the projects use interfacing such as Pellon 931TD Fusible Midweight.

Minki likes to cut the interfacing ¼˝ smaller than the fabric to keep it out of the seam allowance—this results in nice, crisp, clean edges. However, this is optional. Feel free to cut the interfacing the same size as the fabric, using the patterns, if you prefer.

For heavier-weight interfacing, try fast2fuse HEAVY Interfacing (by C&T Publishing).

MAKE A TEMPLATE

If you think you will make a project more than once, make a template of the pattern piece. You don't need anything special to make templates; a recycled cereal box or file folder works just fine. For projects such as the coaster, dessert mat, and tea mat, it is easier to trace a template than to measure the fabric each time, and when you make a stack of them, they are all exactly the same size.

PROJECTS
for the Table

COASTERS

Designed and made by Minki Kim

Finished size: 5˝ × 5˝

Coasters are the perfect small
project to begin your adventures
in sewing illustration. You can
begin with small images, using
thread only, and create a whole
stack of charming works of art for
your home. All you need to start
is a bit of linen and some scraps
of your favorite fabrics. You will
enjoy seeing the coasters in use
around your home, and they also
make wonderful gifts.

For 1 coaster:

LINEN, COTTON PRINTS, AND COTTON BATTING: Scraps (see Cutting for sizes)

FABRIC MARKER: Frixion pen or water-soluble marker

MACHINE SEWING THREAD: Neutral (white or ivory) for piecing and dark 40-weight for outlining

HAND-EMBROIDERY THREAD: Bright and neutral to match linen

HAND-SEWING NEEDLES: Regular and embroidery

CUTTING

LINEN: 1 piece 3⅝″ × 5¾″

COTTON PRINT:
1 piece 2⅝″ × 5¾″ for front
1 piece 5¾″ × 5¾″ for backing

COTTON BATTING:
1 piece 5¾″ × 5¾″

TIP *If you are making multiples, see Make a Template (page 20) and cut out enough fabric for a complete set of coasters and then sew them together assembly-line style.*

INSTRUCTIONS

If you choose different techniques for transferring and appliqué than those used here, the materials and steps may vary slightly from those described in this project. Refer to Basic Techniques (page 6) for instruction on all the different methods.

Seam allowances are ¼″ unless otherwise noted.

MAKE THE COASTER TOP

Place the cotton print for the front of the coaster and the linen right sides together and sew along a long edge. Press the seam allowance toward the print side.

SEWING ILLUSTRATION

Transfer technique shown: Frixion pen.

1. Transfer the Coaster design (page 25) of your choice using your method of choice (see Transferring a Design to Fabric, page 6).

2. Place the batting on the wrong side of the coaster front. Having the batting underneath stabilizes the design as you sew.

3. Prepare your machine with an open-toe appliqué foot (if you have one) and dark thread. Set the stitch length to about 1.6.

4. Start on one of the larger elements in the design—in this case, on the long edge of the coffee pot. Carefully sew along the design.

Remember, it doesn't have to be perfect; that's part of the charm.

5. Hand stitch a few little cross-stitches with 2 strands of embroidery thread in red or a color that complements the cotton print fabric.

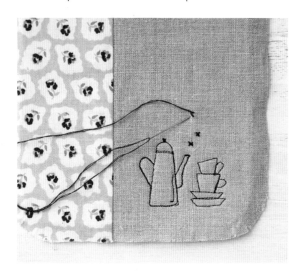

FINISH IT UP

1. Use something round (the round end of a 1½˝ spool of thread works well) to mark rounded corners onto both the front and back pieces of the coaster. Trim.

2. Place the coaster front and back right sides together and pin. Sew around the coaster, leaving about 2½˝ open along the straight side with the cotton print.

3. Turn the coaster right side out and press flat. Use a chopstick or other similar object to help push out the corners to make them perfectly round. Turn under the seam allowance for the opening and press well. Hand stitch the opening closed.

ADD EMBELLISHMENTS

1. Thread an embroidery needle with 2 strands of embroidery thread. Stitch around the edge of the coaster, about ⅛″ from the edge, with a running stitch. Alternatively, topstitch around the coaster using your sewing machine. If you are having trouble keeping the stitching straight, see Straight Stitching (page 18).

2. If you are hand stitching, bury the knot so that it doesn't show on the back (see Hand Embroidery, page 18).

Enjoy your new coaster with a cup of coffee or tea. You deserve it!

Coaster designs
(For iron-on transfer, see pullout page P1.)

TEA MAT

Designed and made by Minki Kim | Finished size: 8½˝ × 6˝

We love tea mats. They are the perfect size for a cup of tea or coffee and a little sweet treat. They are quick to sew up and make perfect gifts. Tea mats give your home a cozy, handmade look and just may inspire you to bake up a batch of scones and invite a friend over for a cup of tea and a chat.

For 1 tea mat:

NEUTRAL COTTON OR LINEN, COTTON PRINTS, AND COTTON BATTING: Scraps (see Cutting for sizes)

FUSIBLE WEB: such as Steam-A-Seam

FABRIC MARKER: Frixion pen or water-soluble marker

MACHINE SEWING THREAD: Neutral (white or ivory) for piecing and dark 40-weight for outlining

HAND-EMBROIDERY THREAD: 1 color to contrast with cotton front

HAND-SEWING NEEDLES: Regular and embroidery

CUTTING

NEUTRAL COTTON: 1 piece 6½˝ × 9˝ for front

COTTON PRINT: 1 piece 6½˝ × 9˝ for back

BATTING: 1 piece 6½˝ × 9˝

INSTRUCTIONS

If you choose different techniques for transferring and appliqué than those used here, the materials and steps may vary slightly from those described in this project. Refer to Basic Techniques (page 6) for instruction on all the different methods.

Seam allowances are ¼˝ unless otherwise noted.

SEWING ILLUSTRATION

Transfer technique shown: Fusible web. Refer to the package for instructions on how to use your brand of fusible web. Remember to reverse the designs when using fusible web.

1. Transfer one of the Tea Mat designs (page 29) to the print fabric scraps using your method of choice (see Creating Fabric Accents, page 14).

2. Cut the fabric accents out on the traced lines.

3. Fuse the accents to the front fabric piece.

4. Sketch in the details of the design, such as the string and front rim of the saucer.

5. Layer the tea mat top onto the batting. If you used fusible web to attach the teacups, you do not need to secure the accents with stitching. If you didn't use fusible web, secure each accent shape by stitching about ⅛″ away from the edge with neutral-color thread and a stitch length of 1.6. Use an open-toe appliqué foot if you have one.

6. Thread the sewing machine with dark thread and set the stitch length to 1.6. Stitch around the edge of the design and along the detail markings.

TIP *Clipping the seam allowance in the corners helps create sharper corners. Be careful not to clip the stitches!*

FINISH IT UP

1. Sew together the tea mat back and front, right sides together, leaving a 3″ opening along a side. Clip the corners.

2. Turn the tea mat right side out, using a chopstick or other similar object to help poke the corners out neatly. Press flat. Turn under the seam allowance for the opening and press well. Hand stitch the opening closed.

ADD EMBELLISHMENTS

Thread an embroidery needle with 2 strands of embroidery thread. Stitch around the edge of the coaster, about ¼″ from the edge, with a running stitch. If you are having trouble keeping your stitching straight, see Straight Stitching (page 18). Skip over the corners. Add small X's to each of the corners. Be sure to bury any knots so they don't show on the back (see Hand Embroidery, page 18).

Now invite a friend over for tea to enjoy your little work of art.

Tea Mat designs
(For iron-on transfer, see pullout page P1.)

DESSERT MAT

Designed and made by Minki Kim

Finished size: 11˝ × 11˝

We love the unusual size of this dessert mat. Its square dimensions give it a bit of flair and allow plenty of room for the most important part of the meal—dessert! Whatever your dessert preference (Minki loves cheesecake with black coffee, while Kristin prefers anything chocolate and a latte), you will find yourself making these charming mats for all your family and friends. Hand quilting encourages you to slow down and savor the process of creating, just as you will savor the treats that will be served on the dessert mat when you are done.

LINEN, COTTON PRINTS FOR BACKING AND APPLIQUÉ, AND COTTON BATTING: Scraps in various sizes and colors

COTTON PRINT: ¼ yard for binding

COTTON LACE TRIM: ⅜ yard

COTTON RIBBON TAG: (optional)

GLUE STICK OR PEN

FABRIC MARKER: Frixion pen or water-soluble marker

MACHINE SEWING THREAD: Neutral (white or ivory) for piecing and dark 40-weight for outlining

HAND-EMBROIDERY THREAD: Embroidery floss, perle cotton, or hand-quilting thread; variegated

HAND-SEWING NEEDLES: Regular and hand quilting (optional)

CUTTING

LINEN: 1 piece 11¾″ × 11¾″

COTTON PRINT:
1 piece 11¾″ × 11¾″ for backing

5 strips 1¾″-wide cut on the bias (totaling 54″) for binding (See Making and Using Single-Fold Bias Binding, page 33.)

QUILT BATTING:
1 piece 11¾″ × 11¾″

COTTON LACE TRIM: 1 piece 11¾″ long (optional)

INSTRUCTIONS

If you choose different techniques for transferring and appliqué than those used here, the materials and steps may vary slightly from those described in this project. Refer to Basic Techniques (page 6) for instruction on all the different methods.

Seam allowances are ¼″ unless otherwise noted.

SEWING ILLUSTRATION

Transfer technique shown: Frixion pen.

1. Transfer one of the Dessert Mat designs (page 34) to the cotton scraps using your method of choice (see Transferring a Design to Fabric, page 6).

2. Cut out all the fabric accent pieces (see Creating Fabric Accents, page 14).

3. Mark an 11″ × 11″ square centered on the linen. Trace around a rounded object such as a 1½″ spool to create rounded corners. This is the final size of the project, and having the marked lines will help you decide where to place your design. *Do not trim the linen yet*—you'll be handling the fabric quite a bit, and linen tends to fray when handled.

4. Glue the fabric accents in place. You can place them anywhere that seems pleasing to you or as follows: the top of the design is 5½″ from the bottom edge of the mat, and the right edge of the design is about 1¼″ from the right edge of the mat. Transfer the wire rack image using your method of choice (see Transferring a Design to Fabric, page 6). You may be able to just sketch it in yourself. Remember, it doesn't have to be perfect!

5. Place the batting underneath the dessert mat top. The batting underneath will stabilize the design as you sew.

6. Thread your sewing machine with neutral thread and set the stitch length to about 1.6. Use an open-toe appliqué foot if you have one.

7. Secure the fabric accents to the background by stitching about ⅛″ inside the edge of each piece. Stitch a little meander pattern inside the frosting accents for extra detail.

8. Thread the sewing machine with dark thread. Stitch around each fabric accent, very close to the edge. Outline each piece once or twice, depending on the level of contrast you want. Clip the threads. In this design, don't do any outlining with dark thread on the white frosting elements. Lastly, stitch the rack design and the angle on the corner of the box of berries. Your sewing illustration won't look exactly the same as mine but will be beautifully and uniquely yours.

MAKE THE DESSERT MAT TOP

1. If you are using cotton lace, pin it in place about 2¼″ up from the bottom of the mat. If desired, add a cotton ribbon tag. Turn the right-hand end of the ribbon under and stitch close to the edge to secure it. Position the tag under the trim so that the top edge will be stitched down as you sew the trim down, and make sure that the left edge of the tag will be stitched into the seam allowance. Stitch the trim in place.

2. Use a ruler and a temporary marking pen to mark a crosshatch pattern on the top of the dessert mat, with lines 1½″ apart. Draw the first line diagonally from corner to corner and then continue marking every 1½″. **Do not mark over the sewing illustration and trim areas.**

FINISH IT UP

1. Layer the dessert mat top and the backing, wrong sides together. Thread or pin baste. Baste well to avoid creating pleats in the backing.

2. Hand quilt using variegated thread. Use 2 strands of variegated thread for a thicker line. To match the colors, cut a long piece of thread, fold it in half, and adjust until the colors match. Thread your needle and knot both strands together. Start stitching in a corner and sew a running stitch from corner to corner, beginning and ending just inside the seam allowance. Then stitch from corner to corner in the opposite direction. Continue working in this manner from the center outward.

TIP *Hand sewing is charming, but feel free to machine quilt if you prefer. If you do hand quilt this mat, embroidery floss, perle cotton, and hand-quilting thread are all great choices.*

3. Trim the entire project on the drawn outline.

4. Create 54˝ of bias binding from the strips and finish the mat (see Making and Using Bias Binding, at right). *Note: It's important to use* bias *binding because of the rounded corners.*

Now it's time to make a lovely dessert and enjoy your new project!

MAKING AND USING BIAS BINDING

1. *Cut strips the indicated width at a 45° angle to the selvages.*

2. *Sew the binding strips together on the diagonal to achieve the needed length. Press the seams open.*

3. *Fold the binding strip in half lengthwise, wrong sides together, and press.*

4. *Open up the strip and fold a raw long edge up to the center crease and press. Repeat with the second long raw edge.*

5. *Open up the folds. Leaving the first few inches free, start sewing the binding to the right side of the project by aligning the raw edge of the binding with the raw edge of the project. Sew along the fold (about ⅜˝).*

6. *Sew all the way around, stopping a few inches from the starting point.*

7. *Overlap the starting end over the binding at the stopping point. Mark a diagonal line.*

8. *Add ½˝ total for seam allowances, cut the binding tail, and sew together the ends on the diagonal with a ¼˝ seam allowance. Press the seam open.*

9. *Fold the binding to the wrong side, fold under the raw edge, and stitch down by hand.*

Dessert Mat designs
(For iron-on transfer, see pullout page P1.)

PROJECTS
for the Crafter

PINCUSHION

Designed and made by Minki Kim

Finished size: 2¾˝ × 2¾˝

We see these little beauties as pincushions, and they can be, but they can also be so much more. One can also be the perfect ornament for a crafty friend, a little backpack decoration for a special child, or an adorable embellishment to a wrapped gift. The possibilities are endless! Minki used to have a whole basketful of them, but it has dwindled down to almost nothing as she has found so many occasions to give them away. As a matter of fact, she is working right now to fill that basket back up with a new batch of these little gems.

For 1 pincushion:

LINEN, COTTON PRINTS FOR BACKING AND APPLIQUÉ, AND EMBROIDERY BACKING PAPER OR STABILIZER: Small scraps

POLYFILL: Small amount

MATERIAL FOR HANGING LOOP: ¼ yard (optional; leather cord or strip, baker's twine, elastic band, and ribbon are all good choices)

FABRIC MARKER: Frixion pen or water-soluble marker

MACHINE SEWING THREAD: Neutral (white or ivory) for piecing and dark 12-weight for outlining

HAND-SEWING NEEDLES: Regular

CUTTING

You may need to adjust the cut size for larger motifs.

LINEN: 1 square 3¼˝ × 3¼˝

COTTON PRINT: 1 square 3¼˝ × 3¼˝ for backing

EMBROIDERY BACKING PAPER OR STABILIZER: 1 square 2˝ × 2˝

MATERIAL FOR HANGING LOOP: 1 piece 7˝ long (optional)

INSTRUCTIONS

If you choose different techniques for transferring and appliqué than those used here, the materials and steps may vary slightly from those described in this project. Refer to Basic Techniques (page 6) for instruction on all the different methods.

Seam allowances are ¼˝ unless otherwise noted.

SEWING ILLUSTRATION

Transfer technique shown: Fusible web (remember to reverse the designs), so there will be no need to secure the fabric with additional stitching with white thread. Draw in the additional spool and thread detail with a temporary marking pen.

1. Transfer the one of the Pincushion designs (page 39) using your method of choice (see Creating Fabric Accents, page 14).

TIP *Fussy cutting the fabric on the sewing machine adds a cute touch. Minki chooses fabrics with prints in a scale appropriate to the size of the design.*

2. Place the embroidery backing paper or stabilizer underneath the linen to stabilize the design as you sew.

3. Thread your sewing machine with brown thread. Set the stitch length to 1.6 and use an open-toe appliqué foot if you have one.

4. Stitch around each fabric accent, very close to the edge. Outline each piece once or twice, depending on the level of contrast you desire. Don't forget to stitch the spool and thread details.

FINISH IT UP

1. If you are making a hanging loop, fold whatever you are using in half. Position the loop centered at the top of the right-side-up linen piece, aligning the raw edges with the raw edges of the fabric. Sew back and forth over the loop, close to the edge, to secure it.

2. Place the pincushion top and back right sides together. Sew around the outside, leaving a 1½″ opening on a side for turning. Make sure the loop is between the front and backing fabrics.

3. Turn the pincushion right side out, using a chopstick or similar object to gently poke out the corners. Press well. Stuff with polyfill until quite firm. Hand stitch the opening closed, using a slip stitch.

Stitch up your own basketful of these fun little trinkets and decide whether to give them away or keep them for yourself.

   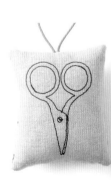

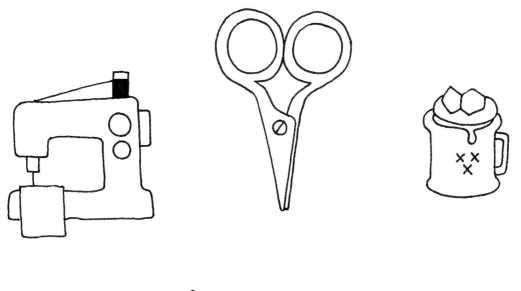

Pincushion designs
(For iron-on transfer, see pullout page P1.)

NEEDLE CASE

Designed and made by Minki Kim | Finished size: 9½″ × 4″ open, 3″ × 4″ closed

Needle cases are such quick and useful projects—they have such a long history, back to a time when hand sewing was more common than it is today. Projects in this book use several different types of needles: hand sewing, quilting, and embroidery. This sweet bifold needle case will help keep them organized, making sewing even more enjoyable. Since the motifs are larger, it makes a great beginner project. Every sewer and crafter in your life will appreciate one, but don't forget to make one for yourself!

LINEN, COTTON PRINTS, EMBROIDERY BACKING PAPER OR STABILIZER, FELT, AND BATTING: Scraps (see Cutting for sizes)

NARROW/DECORATIVE ELASTIC: ⅛ yard

½″-WIDE COTTON RIBBON: ⅛ yard (optional)

BUTTON: 1

FABRIC MARKER: Frixion pen or water-soluble marker

MACHINE SEWING THREAD: Neutral (white or ivory) for piecing, red and dark 12-weight for outlining

HAND-EMBROIDERY THREAD: 1 color to contrast with cotton print and neutral to match linen

HAND-SEWING NEEDLES: Regular and embroidery

CUTTING

LINEN: 1 piece 4″ × 4½″ for the outer front and 1 piece 3½″ × 4½″ for the inside fold

COTTON PRINTS: 1 piece 3½″ × 4½″ for outer back, 1 piece 10″ × 4½″ for inside, and 1 piece 4″ × 4½″ for pocket

EMBROIDERY BACKING PAPER: 2 pieces 2½″ × 3″

BATTING: 1 piece 10″ × 4½″

FELT: 1 piece 9″ × 3½″

ELASTIC: 1 piece 3″ long

½″-WIDE COTTON RIBBON: 1 piece 4½″ long

INSTRUCTIONS

If you choose different techniques for transferring and appliqué than those used here, the materials and steps may vary slightly from those described in this project. Refer to Basic Techniques (page 6) for instruction on all the different methods.

Seam allowances are ¼″ unless otherwise noted.

SEWING ILLUSTRATION

Transfer technique shown: Frixion pen.

1. Transfer the Needle Case designs (page 44) to the linen pieces using your desired method (see Transferring a Design to Fabric, page 6).

2. Add embroidery backing paper or stabilizer under the fabric to stabilize the design as you stitch.

3. Thread your sewing machine with dark thread (the 12-weight thread gives it a bold look). Set the stitch length to 1.6 and use an open-toe appliqué foot if you have one. Outline the design carefully, going slowly around the curves. Change to red thread and follow the outline of the pin and fill in the heart shape.

MAKE THE OUTSIDE

1. Fold the elastic piece in half, making a loop. Center the loop on the right-hand side of the smaller linen piece as shown, with the raw edges aligned. Sew back and forth over the elastic, close to the edge, to secure it.

TIP *Sewing through thin elastic can be tricky. Once you have the raw edges of the elastic aligned with the edge of the fabric, and the linen in place on top, try sewing back and forth over just the elastic area a couple of times. That will secure the elastic, and then you can go ahead and stitch the seam without worrying about the elastic shifting around.*

----

2. Sew the linen pieces to either side of the 3½″ × 4½″ cotton print piece—the smaller piece on the left and the larger piece on the right. Press.

3. Pin the batting to the wrong side of the completed outside piece.

4. Pin and stitch the cotton ribbon over the seam on the right side of the outside piece, sewing close to each edge.

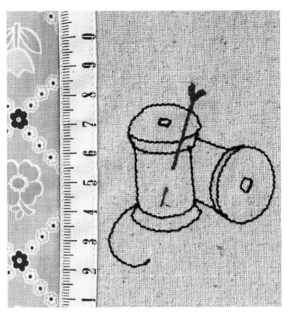

MAKE THE POCKET

1. Fold the pocket fabric in half so that it measures 4″ × 2¼″.

2. Baste the pocket to the lower left corner of the inside fabric piece inside the seam allowance, aligning the raw edges on the 2 outer sides.

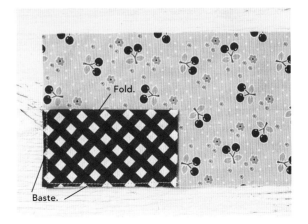

PUT IT TOGETHER

1. Pin together the outside and inside, right sides together.

2. Sew together, leaving a 2½″ opening along a side. Clip the corners.

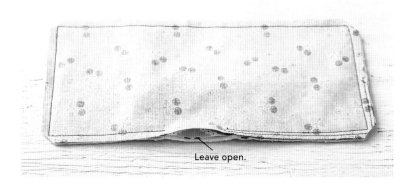

Leave open.

FINISH IT UP

1. Turn right side out, using a chopstick or other similar object to poke the corners out neatly. Press flat. Turn the seam allowance for the opening under and press well. Hand stitch the opening closed, using a slip stitch.

2. Place the felt on the inside and center it with about a ¼″ border on all sides. Pin to secure. Sew the felt to the needle case by stitching along each side of the cotton ribbon and again along the seam between the back and inside flap.

3. Sew the button on the front panel, using the elastic loop to mark the placement. Make sure that the thread doesn't go through to the inside fabric, but just goes through the linen. This will give you a nicer finish.

4. Using 1–2 strands of embroidery floss in a contrasting color, stitch around the outside edge of the needle case, about ⅛″ from the edge, using a running stitch.

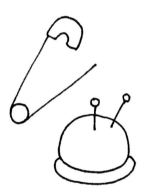

Needle Case designs
(For iron-on transfer, see pullout page P1.)

You just might need to fill this up with some brand-new sharp sewing needles as a little treat for yourself.

NOTIONS BASKET

Designed and made by Minki Kim | Finished size: 6˝ wide × 3½˝ high × 5˝ deep

Don't you love including little inspiring sayings in your projects? They bring a smile every time you see them. We're sure you'll want to keep this little notions basket nearby whenever you are sewing or knitting or indulging any of your creative pursuits. And hopefully its little message will remind you to take time every day to do something that makes you happy.

MATERIALS AND SUPPLIES

LINEN: ¼ yard

COTTON PRINT SCRAPS:
Various sizes and colors

LINING FABRIC: ⅜ yard

**EMBROIDERY BACKING PAPER
OR STABILIZER:** Scraps

**BATTING OR FUSIBLE STIFF
INTERFACING (SUCH AS FAST2FUSE
LIGHT, BY C&T PUBLISHING, OR
71F PELTEX):** ⅓ yard for exterior

**FUSIBLE MIDWEIGHT INTERFACING
(SUCH AS PELLON 931TD):**
20″ wide, ⅓ yard for lining

KRAFT•TEX (BY C&T PUBLISHING):
½″-wide strips, total of 31″
or **LEATHER:** ½″-wide strips,
total of 15½″

BRADS OR DOUBLE CAP RIVETS:
4 (optional, to attach handles)

BUTTONS: 3 (optional)

**WASH-AWAY STABILIZER (SUCH AS
WASH-AWAY STITCH STABILIZER, BY
C&T PUBLISHING):** 1 sheet

FABRIC MARKER: Frixion pen
or water-soluble marker

MACHINE SEWING THREAD: Neutral
(white or ivory) for piecing and
dark 40-weight for outlining

HAND-EMBROIDERY THREAD:
Complementary to the
cotton print and red

HAND-SEWING NEEDLES:
Regular and embroidery

CUTTING

LINEN: 4 squares 3½″ × 3½″ for sides, 1 piece 2¾″ × 3½″ for pocket, and 1 piece 5½″ × 6½″ for base

COTTON PRINT SCRAPS: 1 square 3½″ × 3½″ for pocket and 4 pieces 2″ × 2½″ (2 light and 2 dark) and 8 squares 2″ × 2″ (4 light and 4 dark) for patchwork

LINING FABRIC: 1 piece, using the Notions Basket pattern (page 53)

EMBROIDERY BACKING PAPER OR STABILIZER: 3 squares 3″ × 3″

BATTING OR FUSIBLE STIFF INTERFACING: 1 piece for exterior, using the Notions Basket pattern (page 53)

FUSIBLE MIDWEIGHT INTERFACING: 1 piece for lining, using the Notions Basket pattern (page 53)

KRAFT•TEX: 4 pieces ½″ × 7¾″
or **LEATHER:** 2 pieces ½″ × 7¾″

Side 2

INSTRUCTIONS

If you choose different techniques for transferring and appliqué than those used here, the materials and steps may vary slightly from those described in this project. Refer to Basic Techniques (page 6) for instruction on all the different methods.

Seam allowances are ¼″ unless otherwise noted.

SEWING ILLUSTRATION

Transfer technique shown: Wash-away stabilizer.

1. Transfer the Notions Basket designs (page 52) to 3 of the 3½″ × 3½″ linen squares using your desired method (see Transferring a Design to Fabric, page 6). Back each piece with embroidery backing paper or stabilizer.

2. Thread your sewing machine with dark thread. Set the stitch length to 1.6 and use an open-toe appliqué foot if you have one. Outline each design once or twice, depending on the level of contrast you desire.

3. Hand embroider the word "Sew" using 2 strands of red embroidery floss.

4. If you are using wash-away stabilizer, rinse it away under cool running water and set the piece aside to dry.

TIP *Adding embroidery backing paper or stabilizer underneath the sewing illustration area gives the stitching a bit more stability—it helps even when using wash-away stabilizer on the top of the fabric.*

TIP *When you iron the fabric after using wash-away stabilizer, always cover your project with a press cloth, so that if there is any glue or stabilizer remaining it won't stick to your iron.*

MAKE THE EXTERIOR

MAKE THE PATCHWORK

1. Sew 1 light 2˝ × 2½˝ piece and 1 dark 2˝ × 2½˝ piece together along the longer sides, right sides together, to make a two-patch unit. Repeat with the other 2 patches of the same size. Press the seams toward the dark fabric. Set aside.

2. Repeat Step 1 with the 2˝ × 2˝ squares to make 4 pairs.

3. Sew together 2 pairs from Step 2, nesting the seams and alternating the placement of the dark and light squares to make a four-patch unit. Repeat with the remaining units.

MAKE THE POCKET

1. Sew the 3½˝ × 3½˝ pocket lining to the 2¾˝ × 3½˝ linen pocket front. Press the seam toward the lining. Fold the lining over the linen to cover the seam allowance, aligning the bottom edges. Press.

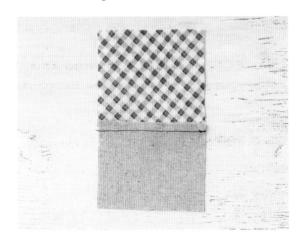

2. Place the pocket front on the remaining 3½˝ × 3½˝ linen square, aligning the bottom edges. Pin in place. Set aside.

ASSEMBLE THE SIDES AND BASE

1. Stitch a two-patch unit to the left-hand side of an embroidered linen square to make Side 2. Press the seam allowance toward the two-patch. Repeat this step to make Side 4 using the assembled pocket square.

2. Stitch a four-patch unit to the right-hand side of each of the units from the previous step. Press the seam allowance toward the four-patch. These will be part of Sides 1 and 3.

3. Stitch an embroidered linen square to the left-hand side of each of the units from the previous step. These will be the other half of Sides 1 and 3.

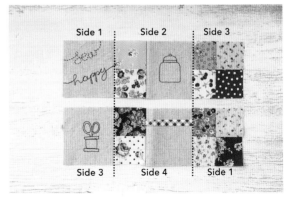

ATTACH THE BASE

1. Pin the 5½″ × 6½″ linen piece to the Side 1/2/3 unit, centering the 5½″ side of the linen piece on the Side 2 unit. Stitch together, starting and ending ¼″ in from each end of the linen bottom (this should align with the seams on the side panels). Press the seam allowance toward the bottom piece.

2. Repeat Step 1 to sew the Side 3/4/1 unit to the opposite side of the bottom piece.

Don't sew final ¼″.

Don't sew final ¼″.

1. Baste or fuse the corresponding outer batting/interfacing piece, centered, to the wrong side of the unit just completed. The interfacing will be inset ¼″ on each side except for the basket's top edges will be free of interfacing. If you are using a double-sided fusible interfacing, make sure to protect your ironing board and iron.

2. From the right side, topstitch or machine quilt around each patch as desired.

3. Fold the capital letter "I"-shaped unit in half, matching up the Side 1 pieces right sides together, so that the top and bottom of the "I" meet at the short ends. Pin and stitch together.

4. Flatten the side you just sewed and align it with the edge of the base, centering the side seam. Sew, making sure to lock your stitches at the beginning and end of the seam for strength.

5. Repeat Steps 3 and 4 on the opposite side.

MAKE THE LINING

1. Fuse the lining interfacing to the wrong side of the lining fabric. There will be a 1″ unlined section on each wide end.

2. Repeat Finish the Exterior, Steps 3–5 (page 49), to sew the lining together.

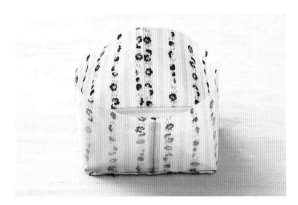

PUT IT TOGETHER

1. Turn the outer basket right side out, poking out each corner. Place the lining inside the outer basket, wrong sides together. Fold the top edge of the lining to the inside, leaving ½″ showing on the exterior of the basket. Pin and press.

2. Hand stitch the lining in place, using a running stitch and 2 strands of embroidery floss.

Side 3

1. If you are using kraft•tex, make the handles by stacking
2 pieces of kraft•tex and topstitching close to each long edge to
make 2 handles. If you are using leather, skip this step.

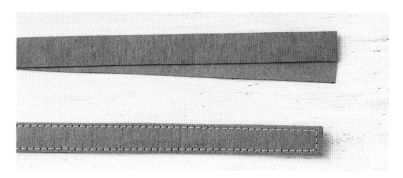

2. Center the handles on the outside of the basket on the short
ends, with the ends of the handles 2½˝ apart. Sew the handles on
or attach them using brads or double cap rivets like Minki did.

3. Embellish the button jar design by hand sewing on buttons if
desired.

*Fill up this little basket with all the notions that you reach for
when enjoying an afternoon of sewing.*

Notions Basket designs
(For iron-on transfer, see pullout page P1.)

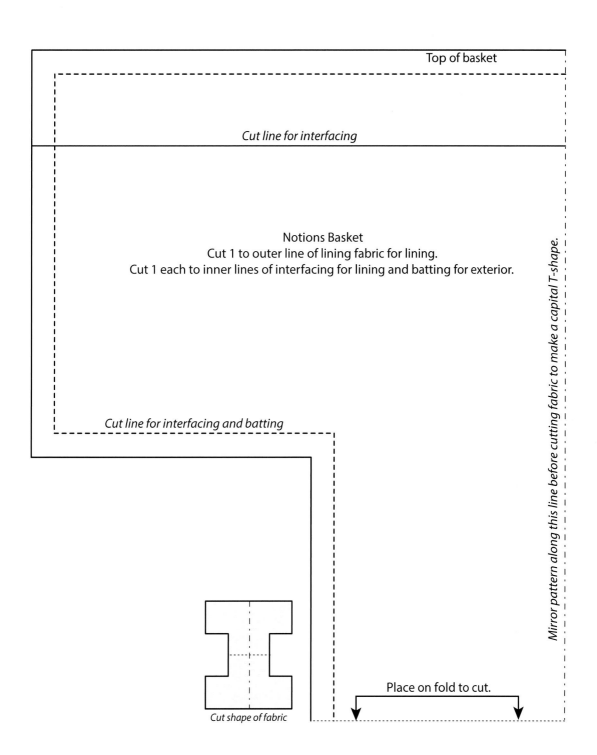

Top of basket

Cut line for interfacing

Notions Basket
Cut 1 to outer line of lining fabric for lining.
Cut 1 each to inner lines of interfacing for lining and batting for exterior.

Cut line for interfacing and batting

Mirror pattern along this line before cutting fabric to make a capital T-shape.

Place on fold to cut.

Cut shape of fabric

PROJECTS
for Every Day

Photo by Minki Kim

PENCIL CASE

Designed and made by Minki Kim

Finished size: 5½˝ × 8½˝

We are stationery-o-holics. We love to see colorful drawing pens and pencils arranged in a mug on a desk. Whether we use them or not, we find them to be inspirational eye candy. Do you feel the same? When you go out, you probably want to take just your favorites, without them being all jumbled together. This case is sturdy enough to keep the pencils neatly organized and easy to find in your purse. You can easily adjust the height and width to fit your favorite pencils. You are sure to find this case as beautiful and useful as we do.

MATERIALS AND SUPPLIES

LINEN: ¼ yard

ASSORTED COTTON PRINT SCRAPS: for back, lining, and flap (See Pencil Case patterns for sizes needed.)

FUSIBLE MIDWEIGHT INTERFACING, (SUCH AS PELLON 931TD): ¼ yard

HEAVYWEIGHT DOUBLE-SIDED STIFF FUSIBLE INTERFACING (SUCH AS FAST2FUSE HEAVY, BY C&T PUBLISHING): 1 piece at least 6″ × 9″

COTTON RIBBON TRIM: Scrap

TAG: 1 (optional)

PAPER-BACKED FUSIBLE WEB

FABRIC MARKER: Frixion pen or water-soluble marker

SEWING MACHINE THREAD: Neutral (white or ivory) for piecing and dark 28-weight for outlining

CUTTING

Note: You may want to create a thin cardboard template for the front, back, and flap patterns. It makes cutting out the fabrics very easy. Recycled cereal boxes or file folders work well.

Use the Pencil Case patterns (pages 60–62).

LINEN: 1 Front and 3 strips 1¾″-wide cut on the bias (totaling 36″) for binding (see Making and Using Bias Binding, page 33)

ASSORTED COTTON PRINT SCRAPS: 2 Flaps (1 exterior and 1 lining), 1 Back and 1 Front for the lining, and 1 Back for the exterior

MIDWEIGHT FUSIBLE INTERFACING: 1 Flap and 2 Fronts (the Flap interfacing pattern is ¼″ smaller all around)

HEAVYWEIGHT DOUBLE-SIDED STIFF FUSIBLE INTERFACING: 1 Back

COTTON RIBBON TRIM: 1 piece 5½″ long

INSTRUCTIONS

Seam allowances are ¼˝ unless otherwise noted.

SEWING ILLUSTRATION

Transfer technique shown: Paper-backed fusible web for the candy fabric accent (remember to reverse the design, unless you are using the iron-on transfer); detail added in with Frixion pen.

If you choose different techniques than those used here, the materials and steps may vary slightly from those described in this project. Refer to Basic Techniques (page 6) for instruction on all the different methods.

1. Transfer one of the Pencil Case designs (page 59 and 60) to the linen Front using your method of choice (see Transferring a Design to Fabric, page 6, and Creating Fabric Accents, page 14).

2. Fuse the midweight interfacing to the wrong side of both Front pieces, matching up the curved corners.

3. Thread your sewing machine with brown thread. Set the stitch length to 1.6 and use an open-toe appliqué foot if you have one.

4. Stitch along the outline of the pencil design. Outline each piece once or twice, depending on the line thickness you desire. Stitch around the fabric accent, very close to the edge, and then stitch in any additional details.

MAKE THE OUTSIDE

1. Sew both fused Front pieces, right sides together, along the top straight edge.

2. Turn right sides out and press. Topstitch about ⅛″ from the top edge.

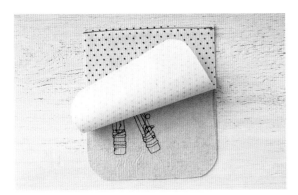

3. Fuse the heavyweight double-sided interfacing to the cotton print exterior Back piece. Fuse the lining Back piece to the opposite side

MAKE THE FLAP

1. Fuse the midweight interfacing flap, centered, on the wrong side of the cotton print outer Flap piece (it will be ¼″ smaller on all sides), matching the curved corners.

2. Pin the cotton ribbon, right side up, ½″ in from the straight edge of the inner Flap. This ribbon will protect the fabric from any marks from pencils inside the case.

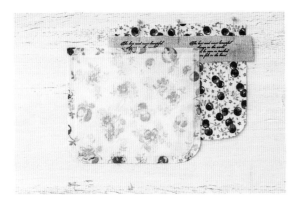

3. Place the inner and outer Flaps right sides together, pin, and sew the sides and the bottom (curved corners). Clip the curved corners.

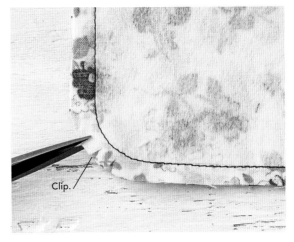

Clip.

4. Turn right side out, gently poke out the corners, and press.

PUT IT TOGETHER

1. Place the front and back pieces together, right sides out and matching the rounded corners, and pin. Tack them together by sewing back and forth about ½″ close to the edge in several places, such as at the top of the pocket, at the corners, and in the center bottom.

2. Center the Flap on top of the Front and Back, right side up, and tack in place along the upper edge and sides. This will hold the project securely as you stitch the binding on.

FINISH IT UP

1. Refer to Making and Using Bias Binding (page 33) to make and sew the 1¾″-wide bias binding to the front side of the pencil case with a ⅜″ seam allowance. Make sure to fold the Flap up and out of the way while stitching. Hand stitch the binding to the back of the pencil case.

2. Hand sew on any embellishments, such as a cute "Carpe Diem" tag, with embroidery thread.

Sharpen your favorite pencils and fill up your new pencil case. Enjoy the simple pleasure of always having your favorites at your fingertips.

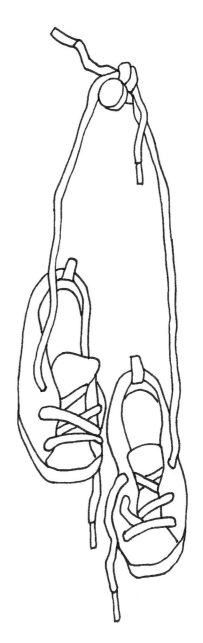

Pencil Case design
(For iron-on transfer, see pullout page P1.)

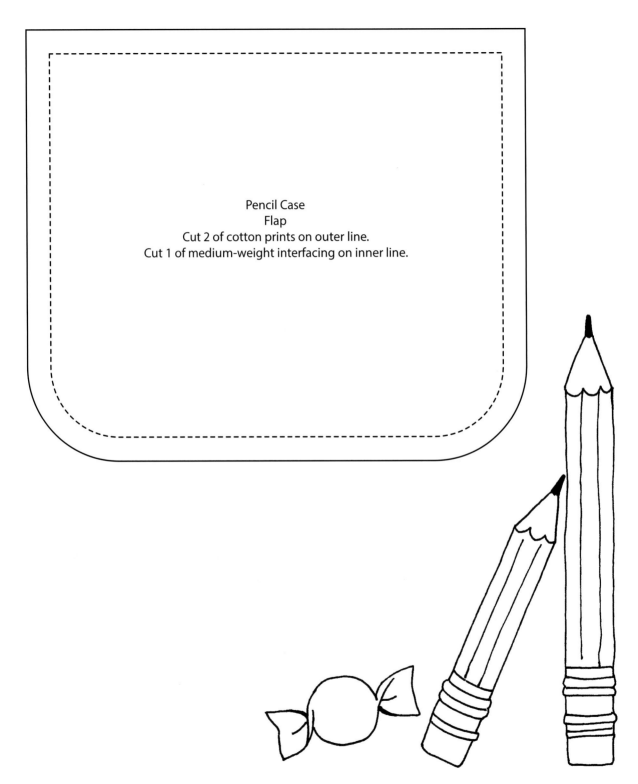

Pencil Case
Flap
Cut 2 of cotton prints on outer line.
Cut 1 of medium-weight interfacing on inner line.

Pencil Case design
(For iron-on transfer, see pullout page P1.)

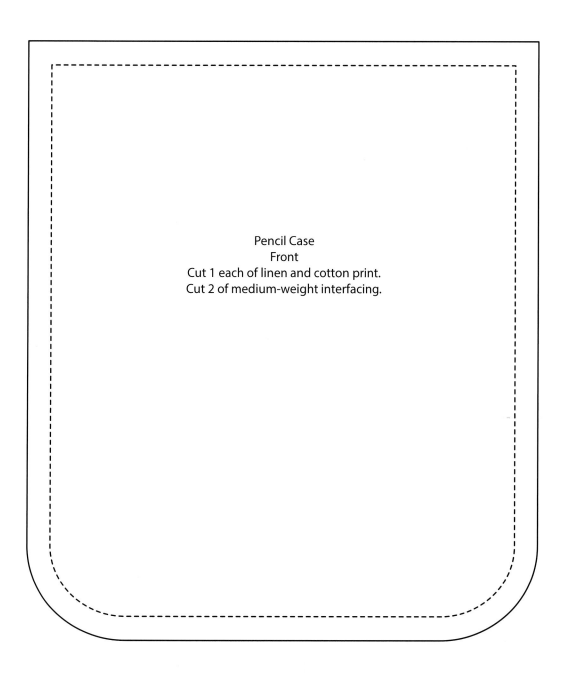

Pencil Case
Front
Cut 1 each of linen and cotton print.
Cut 2 of medium-weight interfacing.

Pencil Case
Back
Cut 2 of cotton prints and 1 of double-sided fusible interfacing.

FABRIC ENVELOPE

Designed and made by Minki Kim | Finished size: 8˝ × 10˝

This darling fabric envelope has a million delightful uses. It's just the right size for an iPad, and the perfect size to store small items such as cords and chargers when you are traveling. Minki made the first one to pass papers back and forth with her daughter's teacher. Much better than a ratty manila envelope! It also makes a wonderful gift with a few goodies tucked inside. We bet you can't make just one!

MATERIALS AND SUPPLIES

LINEN AND COTTON PRINTS:
Scraps for front, back,
flap, and appliqué
(see Cutting for sizes)

LINING FABRIC: ¼ yard or
1 fat quarter

FUSIBLE BATTING: ¼ yard

**FUSIBLE MIDWEIGHT INTERFACING
(SUCH AS PELLON 931TD):** ¼ yard

THIN OR DECORATIVE ELASTIC:
¼ yard

½"-WIDE COTTON RIBBON:
⅓ yard

**PAPER-BACKED FUSIBLE WEB
(SUCH AS STEAM-A-SEAM):**
⅛ yard

BUTTON: 1

FABRIC MARKER: Frixion pen
or water-soluble marker

MACHINE SEWING THREAD:
Neutral (white or ivory)
for piecing and dark
40-weight for outlining

HAND-EMBROIDERY THREAD:
Complementary to
the cotton print

HAND-SEWING NEEDLES:
Regular and embroidery

CUTTING

LINEN: 1 piece 8½" × 11" for front

COTTON PRINT:
1 piece 8½" × 11" for outer back
1 piece 8" × 3¾" for outer flap

LINING: 1 piece 8" × 13¼" and 1 piece 8" × 10½"

FUSIBLE BATTING: 2 pieces 8" × 10"

FUSIBLE MIDWEIGHT INTERFACING: 1 piece 7½" × 12¾",
1 piece 7½" × 9¾", and 1 piece 7½" × 3"

ELASTIC: 1 piece 6" long

COTTON RIBBON: 1 piece 8½" long for the front and
1 piece 3" long for the loop (optional)

INSTRUCTIONS

Seam allowances are ¼" unless otherwise noted.

SEWING ILLUSTRATION

*Transfer technique shown: Paper-backed fusible web (remember
to reverse the designs).*

*If you choose different techniques for transferring and appliqué
than those used here, the materials and steps may vary slightly
from those described in this project. Refer to Basic Techniques
(page 6) for instruction on all the different methods.*

1. Transfer and cut out all the fabric accent pieces using the
Fabric Envelope design (page 67), using your preferred method
(see Creating Fabric Accents, page 14).

TIP *It's fun to fussy cut different elements with this design.
Look for creative fabrics to use for windows and trees.*

----

2. Line up your design about 1¾" from the bottom of the linen
piece and make sure to leave at least ¾" of space on each side.
Fuse the fabric accents to the linen. Sketch in or trace the cloud,
chimney, tree trunks, and windows with a temporary marking pen.

3. Thread your sewing machine with dark thread. Set the stitch length to 1.6 and use an open-toe appliqué foot if you have one. Stitch around each fabric accent, very close to the edge. Outline each piece once or twice, depending on the line thickness you prefer.

4. Stitch the cloud, windows, chimney, and tree trunk details.

TIP *When stitching around a design for sewing illustration, instead of locking your stitches by sewing back and forth, simply sew around the design and overlap your stitching about ¼˝. The stitching will be secure.*

- -

5. Place the cotton ribbon below the row of houses and pin, if desired. Topstitch it in place, about ⅛˝ away from each edge.

MAKE THE OUTSIDE

1. Create round corners by tracing a 1½˝ spool or other round object onto the bottom corners of the front and back pieces, fusible batting, and both lining pieces. Trim the corners.

2. Follow the manufacturer's instructions to fuse a piece of fusible batting to the wrong side of the linen and outer back pieces, centered from side to side and leaving ½˝ of fabric at the top of each.

3. Pin the outer front and back pieces right sides together. Optional: Fold the 3˝ ribbon in half and slip the folded edge in between the 2 pieces, 2˝ down from the top on the right-hand side, as shown. Pin it in place, matching up the raw edges of the ribbon with the raw edges of the fabric.

4. Sew along the sides and bottom, right next to the batting. Do not sew across the top. Clip the curves.

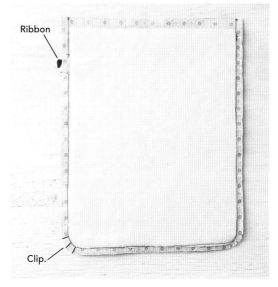

Ribbon

Clip.

5. Turn right side out and press.

MAKE THE LINING

1. Fuse the interfacing, centered, to the wrong side of the corresponding lining pieces and outer flap pieces. For the flap and the smaller lining piece, leave an extra ½˝ of fabric at the top edge only.

2. Align the outside flap piece on top of the large lining piece, right sides together, along the upper 8˝ straight edges. The edge of the flap with ½˝ free of interfacing should be toward the bottom. Pin.

3. Fold the elastic in half to form a loop and knot the cut ends to keep them together. Place the elastic between the flap and lining, centered across the upper edge, with the loop extending about 2˝ inside. Stitch back and forth over the loop within the seam allowance a few times to secure it.

4. Starting and stopping at the interfacing, sew around the flap sides and top—do not sew the lower ½˝ on each side. Trim any excess elastic. Fold the edge of the flap without interfacing up ½˝, wrong sides together, and press.

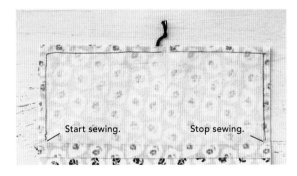

5. Fold the remaining lining over ½˝ toward the wrong side along the top edge and press.

6. Align the 2 lining pieces, right sides together, matching the rounded corners at the bottom. Pin. Sew around the sides and bottom, starting at the lower folded edge and continuing around to the other folded edge. Backstitch at the beginning and end and be careful to keep the flap fabric out of the way.

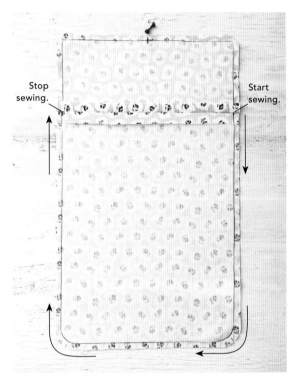

7. Clip the square corners at the top and cut slits into the rounded corners. Turn the flap right side out, carefully poke out the corners, and press the entire piece.

PUT IT TOGETHER

1. Slip the lining inside the outer envelope, with the flap toward the back. Fold the top edge of the outer envelope ½˝ to the wrong side all around. Pin the outer envelope to the lining all along the front, starting at the side seams. Continue pinning along the back, making sure that the extra ½˝ of flap fabric is tucked inside.

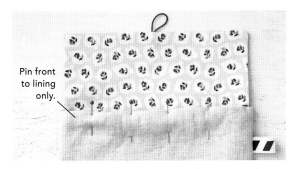

Pin front to lining only.

Slip the lining into the outer envelope. Turn the outer envelope under ½″ and pin to the lining, matching the side seams.

2. Topstich along the top edge of the envelope back, about ⅛″ from the edge. You can continue on to the front to topstitch it as well, or proceed to the next step for a hand finishing option.

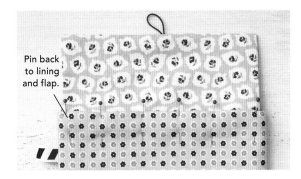

Pin back to lining and flap.

FINISH IT UP

1. To sew the front pieces together, thread an embroidery needle with 2 strands of embroidery floss and sew a running stitch along the front edge.

2. Close the flap and mark the fabric for button placement. Sew on the button.

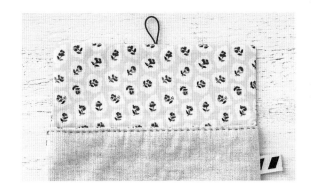

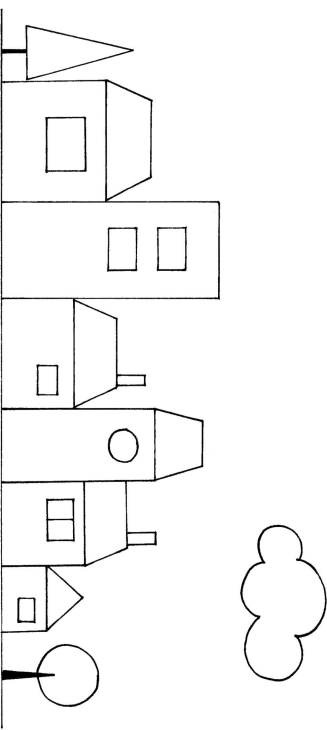

Fabric Envelope design
(For iron-on transfer, see pullout page P1.)

MAKEUP BRUSH CASE

Designed and made by Minki Kim | Finished size: 8½˝ × 10˝ (open)

Despite its name, this little case can be used for many things. But we love the idea of a special place to store makeup brushes, especially when traveling. There are several darling details, such as the flap on top to keep things safely tucked inside and the unique button closure. Whether you use it for makeup brushes, pencils, markers, or crayons for your little ones, we think you will enjoy making and using this adorable case.

LINEN, COTTON PRINTS, AND BATTING: Scraps (see Cutting for sizes)

FUSIBLE MIDWEIGHT INTERFACING (SUCH AS PELLON 931TD): Small scrap

COTTON RIBBON TRIM: ⅜″ wide, ¾ yard

WOODEN TOGGLE BUTTON: 1

FABRIC MARKER: Frixion pen or water-soluble marker

MACHINE SEWING THREAD: Neutral (white or ivory) for piecing and dark 12-weight (such as Aurifil 12/2) for a hand-embroidered look

HAND-QUILTING THREAD: Neutral color to match linen

HAND-SEWING NEEDLES: Quilting and embroidery

TIP *Size this project up or down to make it a perfect fit for your brushes, pencils, or crayons.*

CUTTING

LINEN: 1 piece 5½″ × 10½″ for exterior

COTTON BATTING: 1 piece at least 10″ × 11½″

COTTON PRINTS: Scraps as needed for patchwork (See Make the Patchwork, page 70.)

COTTON PRINT FOR INSIDE: 1 piece 9″ × 10½″ for the pocket and 1 piece 2″ × 9½″ for the flap

LINING FABRIC: 1 piece 9″ × 10½″ and 1 piece 2″ × 9½″ for the flap

FUSIBLE MIDWEIGHT INTERFACING: 1 piece 9″ × 1½″

COTTON RIBBON TRIM: 1 piece 22″ long

INSTRUCTIONS

Seam allowances are ¼″ unless otherwise noted.

PREPARE THE DESIGN

Transfer technique shown: Paper templates and Frixion pen.

If you choose different techniques for transferring and appliqué than those used here, the materials and steps may vary slightly from those described in this project. Refer to Basic Techniques (page 6) for instruction on all the different methods.

Transfer the Makeup Brush Case design (page 73) to the linen using your desired method (see Transferring a Design to Fabric, page 6). The bottom ¼″ of the linen will be covered later, so you may want to place the motif with that in mind.

MAKE THE PATCHWORK

1. Mark horizontal lines ¾″ and 4½″ up from the bottom of the batting, along the 11½″ edge. Mark a vertical line centered between the 2 horizontal lines.

2. Stitch the scraps to the batting, stitch-and-flip style. (Minki starts in the middle and works outward, but you can work in any direction you like. If you wish to stitch horizontally, you must do those sections first, and then add pieces sewn vertically to cover the raw edges.) Cut your scraps the sizes you need as you go. Place the first piece in the center, right side up, on the centerline, as shown, leaving at least a ¼″ seam allowance above and below both horizontal lines.

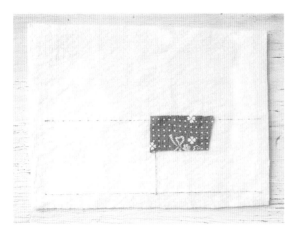

3. Place the next piece right sides together and sew a ¼″ seam, right through the batting. Fold the top piece back and press it flat (finger-pressing works fine).

4. Place the next piece on top of the piece you just sewed, right sides together, and sew. Fold it back and finger-press.

5. Continue in this same manner, working toward the right until you reach the end of the batting.

6. Continue to work from the center section to the left until you reach the end of the batting.

MAKE THE OUTSIDE

Sew the 5½″ × 10½″ linen piece to the patchwork by placing the linen along the top edge of the patchwork, right sides together, across the 10½″ width of the batting. Fold the linen up against the batting and press.

SEWING ILLUSTRATION

Transfer technique shown: Paper templates and Frixion pen.

Thread your sewing machine with brown thread. Set the stitch length to 1.6 and use an open-toe appliqué foot if you have one. Outline each design once or twice, depending on the level of contrast you desire.

TIP *The seam between the patchwork and linen will be covered up with a ribbon, so you can start the sewing illustration a little bit off the linen. Lock your stitches there, and after they are covered with the ribbon, the thicker stitches will not be visible.*

MAKE THE RIBBON CLOSURE

Place the cotton ribbon on the patchwork, along the seam between the patchwork and the linen. Align the edge of the ribbon with the edge of the fabric on the left side. The ribbon will be quite long on the right-hand side. Stitch the ribbon in place with matching thread, along each edge. **Do not sew the final ¼″ on the right-hand side.**

MAKE THE INSIDE

MAKE THE FLAP

1. Center the interfacing on the wrong side of the outer flap piece and fuse in place. Place the 2 flap pieces right sides together and stitch along one long and both short sides, leaving a long side unstitched. Clip the corners.

2. Turn right side out, gently poke out the corners, and press well.

3. Center the flap on the top 10½″ edge of the lining piece and pin in place, aligning the raw edges.

4. Tack the flap in place by sewing back and forth about ½″ at the beginning, middle, and end of the flap, about ⅛″ from the raw edge. This is just to keep it in place as you sew the inside and outside together.

MAKE THE POCKET

1. Fold the pocket fabric in half, so that it is 4½″ × 10½″. Topstitch about ⅛″ away from the folded edge.

2. Mark the sewing lines for the brush dividers on the right side of the pocket. Try marking them about 1″ apart, with 1 channel 2″ wide for a larger brush. Pin the pocket to the lower half of the lining piece, matching the raw edges.

3. Sew along the marked lines to create channels for the brushes. Backstitch at the folded edge to secure the stitches.

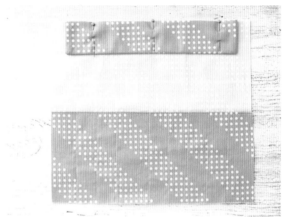

PUT IT TOGETHER

1. Pin the inside (lining/pocket/flap) and outside (linen/patchwork) pieces right sides together, matching all the raw edges. Make sure that the ribbon and flap are both inside. Sew together, leaving a 3″ opening along the bottom edge. Clip the corners and trim off any excess batting.

2. Turn the case right side out, gently poke out the corners, and press. Turn the seam allowance in the opening under, press, and hand stitch closed.

FINISH IT UP

1. Feed the ribbon through the holes on the toggle button, turn the raw edge under, and hand stitch to secure.

2. Using hand-quilting thread, hand quilt a running stitch around each design motif and around the outside of the case.

Fill this sweet case with your favorite brushes, roll it up, wrap the ribbon around it, and tuck the button under the ribbon. You are ready to go!

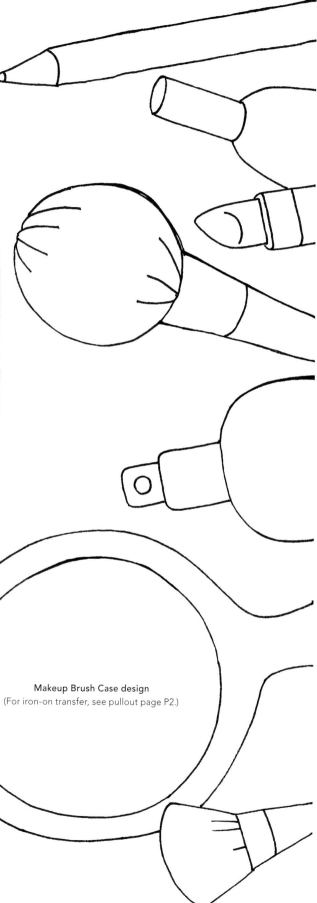

Makeup Brush Case design
(For iron-on transfer, see pullout page P2.)

BAGS FOR
Every Occasion

Photo by Minki Kim

LONG-HANDLED BAG

Designed and made by Minki Kim

Finished size: 14¾˝ × 13˝

Can you ever have too many bags? We both have bags of different sizes and shapes that are all suited for different things. This long-handled bag is perfect for picking up a few items at the market, going on a trip to the bookstore, or packing some things for the park. The handle is long enough to comfortably fit over your shoulder, but feel free to change the length of the handle to suit your own needs. We love the positive message on the typewriter paper, and this is an opportunity to personalize the bag for yourself or someone special. You may find yourself grabbing it each time you head out the door.

LINEN: ½ yard

ASSORTED COTTON PRINTS:
Small and large scraps for
outer bag and fabric accents
(see Cutting for sizes)

LINING FABRIC: ¾ yard

FUSIBLE MIDWEIGHT INTERFACING
(SUCH AS PELLON 931TD):
20˝ wide, 1 yard

EMBROIDERY BACKING PAPER
OR STABILIZER: Small scrap

WASH-AWAY STABILIZER (SUCH AS
WASH-AWAY STITCH STABILIZER,
BY C&T PUBLISHING): 1 sheet

COTTON RIBBON OR LACE:
1 yard

ZIPPER: 7˝ long

FABRIC MARKER: Frixion pen
or water-soluble marker

MACHINE STITCHING THREAD:
Neutral (white or ivory)
for piecing and dark
40-weight for outlining

ZIPPER FOOT FOR SEWING MACHINE

DOUBLE-SIDED FABRIC TAPE:
Wonder Tape (optional)

LINEN: 1 piece 13˝ × 13½˝ for outer front top and
2 pieces 1¾˝ × 34˝ for straps

COTTON PRINT SCRAPS

- **OUTER FRONT BOTTOM PANEL:** 1 piece 3½˝ × 13½˝ and
  2 squares 2˝ × 2˝

- **OUTER BACK TOP:** 1 piece 13˝ × 13½˝

- **OUTER BACK BOTTOM PANEL:** 1 piece 3½˝ × 13½˝ and
  2 pieces 2˝ × 2˝

LINING FABRIC: 2 pieces 13½˝ × 16˝, 1 piece 9˝ × 14˝ for pocket,
and 2 pieces 1¾˝ × 34˝ for straps

FUSIBLE MIDWEIGHT INTERFACING: 2 pieces 13˝ × 14¾˝, 1 piece 4˝ × 8½˝
for pocket, and 2 pieces 1˝ × 34˝ for handles

EMBROIDERY BACKING PAPER OR STABILIZER: 1 piece 5˝ × 6˝

COTTON RIBBON OR LACE: 2 pieces 13½˝ long

INSTRUCTIONS

Seam allowances are ¼˝ unless otherwise noted.

SEWING ILLUSTRATION

Transfer technique shown: Wash-away stabilizer.

*If you choose a different technique than the one used here, the
materials and steps may vary slightly from those described in this
project. Refer to Basic Techniques (page 6) for instruction on all
the different methods.*

1. Transfer the Long-Handled Bag design (page 81) using your
method of choice (see Transferring a Design to Fabric, page 6,
and Creating Fabric Accents, page 14). Cut out the fabric accent
from a scrap.

2. Place embroidery backing paper or stabilizer underneath the
design to stabilize the fabric. If you aren't using fusible web for
the fabric accent, secure it by stitching about ⅛˝ away from the
edge with neutral-color thread and a stitch length of 1.6.

3. Thread your sewing machine with brown thread. Set the stitch length to 1.4 and use an open-toe appliqué foot if you have one. Outline the motif. When stitching the round keys, start at the bottom and overlap the stitching 3–4 stitches. This locks the stitches in place as well as adding a bit of shading to the design.

4. If you are using wash-away stabilizer, rinse under cool running water until the stabilizer dissolves. Lay flat to dry. (You can skip ahead to Make the Invisible Zipper Pocket, page 78, while you wait for it to dry.)

MAKE THE OUTSIDE

1. Sew the print outer front bottom panel to the bottom of the linen piece along the 13½″ edge. Repeat with the back top and bottom pieces.

2. Fuse the corresponding interfacing pieces onto the wrong side of the front and back pieces, leaving 1″ free of interfacing at the top edge and ¼″ on the other 3 sides.

3. Topstitch the cotton lace and/or trim to the front and back pieces, covering up the seam.

MAKE THE INVISIBLE ZIPPER POCKET

Note: If you don't want a pocket inside the bag you can skip this part, but because this bag doesn't have a top closure, an inside zippered pocket will keep your valuables safe. Also, this kind of pocket is a little bit like magic. Don't be afraid to give it a try.

1. Fuse the pocket interfacing, centered, onto the wrong side of a 9″ end of the pocket piece, ¼″ from 3 sides. Mark the zipper opening as shown on the interfacing, ¼″ from the upper edge.

2. Place the pocket piece on top of a piece of the lining fabric, right sides together, centered from side to side with the center zipper line 3″ down from the top of the lining. Pin in place.

TIP *Shhhh! It's okay if you don't like to pin. Try using washi tape or those little red Wonder Clips instead of pins.*

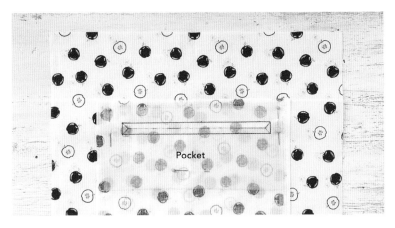

Pocket

3. Sew around the outer marked rectangle. For the cleanest finish, start about halfway down a long side, stitch around the rectangle, and then overlap where you started sewing, by about ½″. No need to backstitch.

4. Cut along the centerline, just to the tip of the marked triangle. Then clip as far as you can into the corners, along the marked lines, making sure not to clip the stitching. An easy way to get the cutting started is to fold the fabric in half and make a small cut on the line right at the fold. Then unfold and continue cutting along the line.

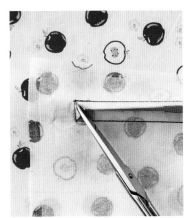

7″

½″

¼″

5. Pull the pocket fabric through the opening to the wrong side of the lining. Press well.

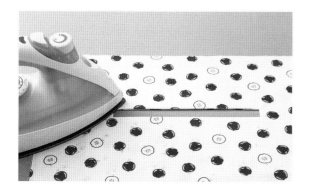

INSTALL THE ZIPPER

1. Tape or pin the zipper in the opening in the lining, both right sides up. Securing the zipper using double-sided fabric tape such as Wonder Tape is easy, but pins work as well.

2. Using a zipper foot, topstitch around the opening about ⅛″ from the edge, through all the layers. As you approach the zipper pull, stop and unzip the zipper about halfway to get the zipper pull out of the way. Then continue stitching.

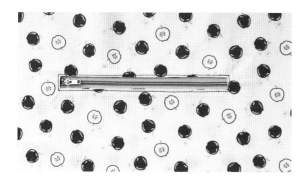

FINISH THE POCKET

Fold the pocket lining in half and stitch around the sides and top. *Be sure to stitch only the pocket closed and not the lining.* Trim away any zipper ends that extend past the sides of the pocket.

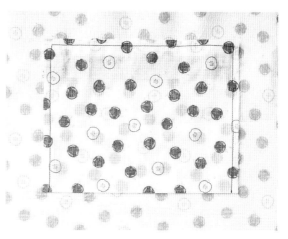

MAKE THE HANDLES

1. Fuse the handle interfacing, centered, to the wrong side of the handle lining.

2. Sew together the linen and lining handle pieces, right sides together, along one long edge.

3. Fold and press ¼″ to the wrong side on the remaining long raw edge of the linen and lining.

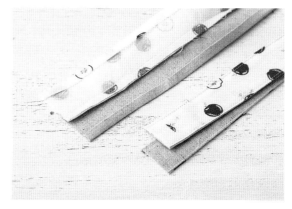

4. Fold the handles in half lengthwise along the seam, with the linen on top and the lining fabric underneath. Press well, making sure that the folded raw edges are inside.

5. Topstitch along each long side, about ⅛″ from the edge. Repeat for the second handle.

ATTACH THE HANDLES AND LINING

1. Mark the top of the outer back piece, 3¼″ in from each side, for the handle placement.

2. Pin 1 handle to the back piece, right sides together, aligning the raw edges at the top and the outer edges of the handle at the 3¼″ marks.

3. Stitch the handle ends in place by sewing across the handle ¾″ from the raw edge and then sewing a rectangle with an X in it to reinforce the handles.

4. Pin the back lining/pocket piece to the back outer piece, right sides together, with the handles sandwiched in between.

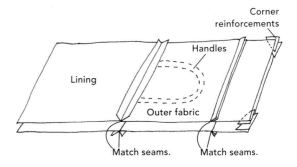

2. Fold the 2″ × 2″ squares in half diagonally, wrong sides together, and press. Slip 2 folded triangles between the 2 layers of the bottom corners of the outer bag, aligning the raw edges and matching the fabrics. Pin in place.

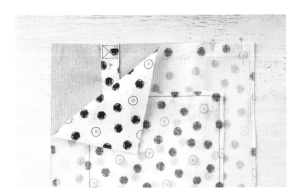

5. Using a 1″ seam allowance, sew the outer and lining pieces together along the top edge.

6. Repeat Steps 1–5 to sew together the outer front bag, lining, and handles.

PUT IT TOGETHER

1. Pin together the front and back bag pieces, right sides together, matching up the outer and lining pieces on top of each other, with the handles sandwiched between the 2 outer pieces. Align the seams and the lace trim as you pin.

Note: These little corner reinforcements will prolong the life of the bag by strengthening the corners.

TIP *Instead of pinning, try tacking the corner reinforcement pieces in place by sewing about ⅛″ from the edge of the fabric in a few places.*

FINISH IT UP

1. Sew around the outside edge of the entire bag, leaving a 4″ opening in the bottom of the lining.

2. Clip the corners and turn right side out.

3. Press well, turning the seam allowance in the opening under. Hand stitch the opening closed.

4. Push the lining inside the bag, pull the handles up, and press the top opening well.

5. Topstitch around the opening, about ⅛″ from the edge.

You may want to make a quick run to the market to try this bag out. Slip your cell phone and wallet into the zipper pocket and off you go!

TODAY IS THE DAY

ROYAL

Long-Handled Bag design
(For iron-on transfer, see pullout page P1.)

DRAWSTRING BAG

Designed and made by Minki Kim | Finished size: 11˝ wide × 11˝ high × 4˝ deep

Picnics at the park will be even more fun when you pack lunch in this adorable insulated bag. You will enjoy creating the hand lettering, and the charming hand-sewn patch on the back will give you a chance to display some of your sewing illustration practice pieces. The ball drawstring closures add a unique and charming touch to a bag that you will find yourself reaching for every day. If you don't pack a lunch, this would be an adorable sewing or knitting bag as well; just substitute cotton batting for the insulated batting.

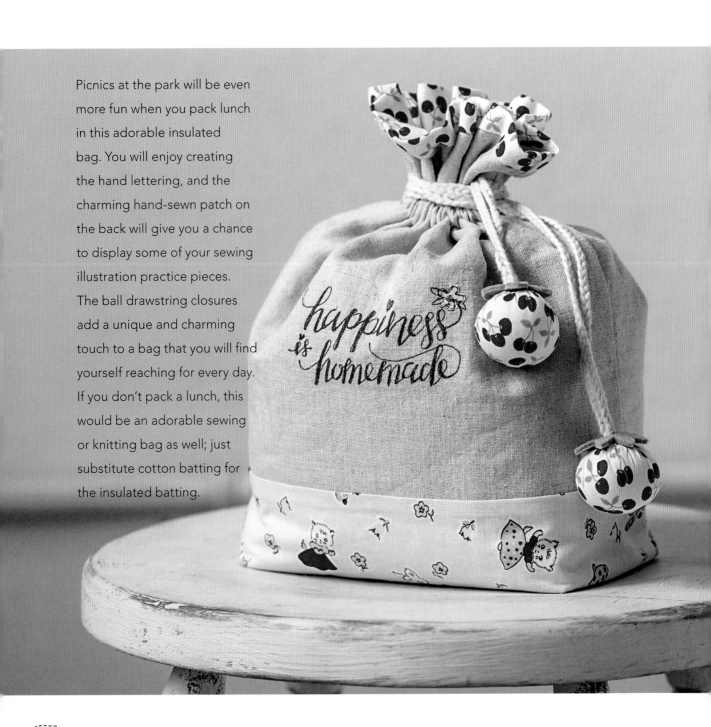

MATERIALS AND SUPPLIES

LINEN: ⅜ yard

COTTON PRINT FOR LINING: ⅜ yard

COTTON PRINT FOR BAG BASE, FABRIC ACCENTS, AND PATCH: Various sizes and colors (see Cutting for sizes)

INSULATED BATTING (SUCH AS INSUL-FLEECE, BY C&T PUBLISHING): ⅜ yard

EMBROIDERY BACKING PAPER OR STABILIZER: 1 piece at least 3″ × 5″ and 1 piece at least 3″ × 4″

FUSIBLE MIDWEIGHT INTERFACING (SUCH AS PELLON 931TD): 20″ wide, ⅜ yard

WASH-AWAY STABILIZER (SUCH AS WASH-AWAY STITCH STABILIZER, BY C&T PUBLISHING): 1 sheet

CORD FOR DRAWSTRING: 1½ yards

POLYFILL: Small amount

FABRIC MARKER: Frixion pen or water-soluble marker

BUTTONS: 2 (optional)

COTTON TRIM: ¾ yard (optional)

GREEN FELT: Small scrap

MACHINE STITCHING THREAD: Neutral (white or ivory) for piecing, red and dark 40-weight for outlining

HAND-SEWING NEEDLES: Regular and embroidery

HAND-SEWING THREAD: Embroidery thread to complement the cotton print, neutral hand-quilting thread

SAFETY PIN FOR THREADING CORD

FABRIC GLUE

CUTTING

LINEN: 2 pieces 9½″ × 11½″ for exterior

COTTON SCRAPS:

- **BAG BASE:** 1 piece 8½″ × 11½″
- **LINING AND DRAWSTRING ENDS:** 1 piece 11½″ × 27¼″ and 2 circles 4″ in diameter
- **PATCH:** 1 piece 3″ × 4″

INSULATED BATTING: 1 piece 11″ × 16″

EMBROIDERY BACKING PAPER OR STABILIZER: 1 piece 3″ × 5″ and 1 piece 3″ × 4″

FUSIBLE MIDWEIGHT INTERFACING: 1 piece 11″ × 16″

CORD FOR DRAWSTRING: 2 pieces 26″ long

COTTON TRIM: 2 pieces 11½″ long (optional)

FELT: 2 leaves from Drawstring Bag designs (page 88)

INSTRUCTIONS

Seam allowances are ¼″ unless otherwise noted.

SEWING ILLUSTRATION

Transfer technique shown: Wash-away stabilizer.

If you choose different techniques for transferring and appliqué than those used here, the materials and steps may vary slightly from those described in this project. Refer to Basic Techniques (page 6) for instruction on all the different methods.

1. Transfer the Drawstring Bag design (Happiness is Homemade, page 88) to one of the linen pieces (see Transferring a Design to Fabric, page 6). Refer to the project photo (page 82) for placement. Place embroidery backing paper or stabilizer under the design area for added stability.

2. Thread your sewing machine with dark thread. Set the stitch length to 1.4 and use an open-toe appliqué foot if you have one. Sew right over the top of the stabilizer, following the design. Make sure to fill in the thicker parts of the letters thoroughly by just stitching back and forth over those areas.

3. Cut out and glue a small flower in place and stitch around the outline. A fussy-cut flower works well here.

4. Change to red thread and stitch the hearts.

TIP *Wash-away stabilizer makes this type of sewing illustration so much easier. You can put a sheet of it in your inkjet printer and copy the design directly onto the stabilizer. Then just peel off the backing and place it in the proper location on the linen.*

5. If you are using wash-away stabilizer, rinse the linen under a faucet with cool water to dissolve the stabilizer. Gently squeeze the excess water out and lay out to dry.

MAKE THE BAG LINING

1. Fold the lining fabric in half, matching the short ends. Cut 2 notches at the corners 2″ wide along the fold by 1¾″ tall to create a 2″ × 3½″ notch in each side of the lining.

2. Fold the insulated batting in half, matching the short ends. Cut 2 notches at the corners 2″ × 2″ along the fold to create a 2″ × 4″ notch in each side of the batting.

3. Place the insulated batting centered on top of the lining, with the shiny side facing the wrong side of the lining. The batting is cut shorter than the lining so that it is less bulky when the drawstrings are pulled tight. Machine quilt a diagonal crosshatch pattern on top of the batting, with lines 1½″ apart, with neutral thread.

4. Sew a strip of cotton trim across the right side of the lining to cover where the quilting stitches end.

MAKE THE OUTER BAG

1. When the fabric with the sewing illustration is dry, press it flat from the *wrong side* (to make sure that any remaining wash-away stabilizer does not get on the iron.)

2. Sew the 2 pieces of linen to each 11½″ side of the bag base. Press the seams toward the center.

3. Fold the outer bag fabric in half, matching the short ends. Cut 2 notches at the corners 2″ wide along the fold by 1¾″ tall to create a 2″ × 3½″ notch in each side of the outer bag.

4. Fold the interfacing in half, matching the short ends. Cut 2 notches at the corners 2″ × 2″ along the fold to create a 2″ × 4″ notch in each side of the insulation.

5. Follow the manufacturer's instructions to fuse the interfacing, centered, to the wrong side of the outer bag fabric. Again, the interfacing is cut shorter than the outer bag so that the top of the bag will gather easily when the drawstrings are pulled tight.

6. With a temporary marking pen, mark sewing lines for the drawstring channel on the right side of the outer bag, 1½″ and 2¼″ from each short end. Mark a second line ¾″ in toward the outer bag from each line. Flip the outer bag over to the wrong side and make the same markings on this side as well.

PUT IT TOGETHER

1. Pin the outer bag to the bag lining, right sides together. Sew each 11½″ end of the bag, but do *not* sew the long, notched sides of the bag yet. Press the seams open.

2. Fold the bag through the center of the notches as shown, aligning the layers of lining and outer fabric, and match up the seams of the bag base. Pin well.

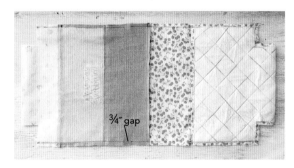

3. Starting at the end of a notch, sew along a long straight side, *stopping at the marked lines for the drawstring channel.* Backstitch a bit when you reach the marked line, then skip the ¾″ gap/opening, and begin sewing again, backstitching at the beginning and end of the seam. Repeat on the opposite side, leaving a 3″ opening along the lining fabric for turning.

CREATE THE BOXED CORNERS

1. Bring the raw edges of a notch together and flatten it out so the fold meets the bag's side seam. Pin and stitch across the raw edges.

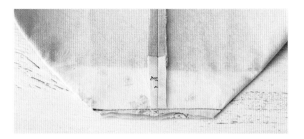

2. Repeat Step 1 to box all 4 notches. This allows the bottom of the bag to stand up by itself.

FINISH IT UP

1. Turn the bag right side out through the opening, making sure to gently poke out all the corners. Press the seam allowance of the opening in and hand stitch it closed using a slip stitch.

2. Push the lining into the bag, leaving ½″ of lining showing at the top. Press.

3. Sew along the marked lines with neutral-color thread to create the drawstring channel. Stitch small X's with 2 strands of embroidery floss (stitch each X twice) at the seam, for added charm and reinforcement.

4. Add buttons to the sides of the bag for an added embellishment, if desired.

MAKE THE DRAWSTRINGS

1. A bit of tape on the cut ends of cord helps reduce fraying. Attach a safety pin to the end of a piece of cord. Starting with the opening on the right side of the bag, thread the cord all the way through the drawstring channel until it comes out the same opening. Repeat to thread the remaining cord through the opening on the left side of the bag.

2. Thread a needle with a long piece of hand-quilting thread (about 24″); bring the ends together and knot, creating a double strand. Turn about ¼″ of fabric over and sew a running stitch around the 4″ circles. Gently pull the thread tight to gather the fabric into a small pouch. Insert the ends of the drawstrings into the pouch and fill with polyfill until quite firm. Pull tight to gather, and stitch the opening closed by hand, stitching through the edge of the ball and through the cords.

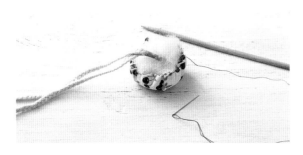

3. Snip to the center of the felt leaf or use a hole punch. Glue the leaf in place on top of the drawstring balls.

MAKE THE SEWING ILLUSTRATION PATCH

Use one of your practice sewing illustration pieces or create a new one.

1. Transfer and cut out all the Drawstring Bag fabric accent pieces (page 88) using your preferred method (see Creating Fabric Accents, page 14). Layer the hamburger pieces on a 3″ × 4″ fabric background, starting with the bottom bun and working upward, and glue them in place. Place a piece of embroidery backing paper or stabilizer under the sewing area for stability.

2. Thread your sewing machine with neutral thread. Set the stitch length to 1.6 and use an open-toe appliqué foot if you have one.

3. Secure the fabric accents to the background by stitching about ⅛″ inside the edge of each piece.

4. Thread your sewing machine with brown thread. Stitch around each fabric accent, very close to the edge. Stitch in the sesame seed detail and any other details.

5. Turn the edges of the patch under ¼″ and press well. Hand stitch it onto the bag with a running stitch, using 2 strands of embroidery floss.

Anyone will love a lunch packed in such a charming bag!

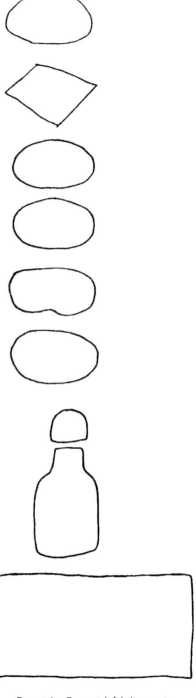

Drawstring Bag design
(For iron-on transfer, see pullout page P1.)

Drawstring Bag leaf design for drawstrings

Drawstring Bag patch pattern
(For all iron-on transfers, see pullout page P1.)

Drawstring Bag patch fabric accents

HOUSE ZIPPER POUCH

Designed and made by Minki Kim | Finished size: 5˝ wide × 4½˝ high × 3½˝ deep

Minki finds little houses magical. Her husband is a woodworker and builds all manner of tables and desks and other useful things for the home. Her girls love to gather up all the bits and pieces of leftover wood and build little houses with them. The houses can be simple or quite elaborate, sometimes involving painting the wood and always requiring tiny pieces of furniture. Fabric being her medium, for this project she wanted to create a fabric house that would capture the magical feeling of these tiny dwellings. It can be a home to all sorts of odds and ends, from small toys, to sewing supplies, to sweet ribbons and hair accessories.

LINEN: 1 piece at least 10″ × 12″

COTTON PRINT: 1 piece at least 8″ × 9″ for outside

COTTON SCRAPS: Various sizes and colors, fussy cutting is encouraged

LINING FABRIC: ⅜ yard or 1 piece at least 11½″ × 16″

FUSIBLE BATTING: ⅜ yard or 1 piece at least 11½″ × 16″ for outside

FUSIBLE MIDWEIGHT INTERFACING (SUCH AS PELLON 931TD): 20″ wide, 1 piece at least 11½″ × 16″ for lining

ZIPPER: 8″ long

COTTON RIBBON: ¼ yard

FABRIC MARKER: Frixion pen or water-soluble marker

MACHINE SEWING THREAD: Neutral (white or ivory) for piecing and dark 40-weight for outlining

HAND-SEWING NEEDLES: Regular

CUTTING

Use the House Zipper Pouch patterns (page 94–96).

LINEN: 1 Body

COTTON PRINT: 2 Tops

LINING FABRIC: 1 Lining

BATTING: 1 Lining

INTERFACING: 1 Lining

COTTON RIBBON: 2 pieces 2½″ long

INSTRUCTIONS

Seam allowances are ¼″ unless otherwise noted.

MAKE THE OUTSIDE

1. Sew the cotton print top pieces to the linen body piece along the 5½″ sides.

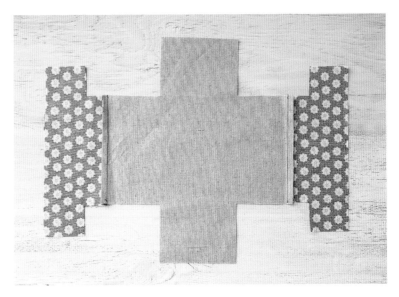

2. Follow the manufacturer's instructions to fuse the batting, centered, to the wrong side.

SEWING ILLUSTRATION

Technique used: Fusible web and Frixion pen.

If you choose different techniques for transferring and appliqué than those used here, the materials and steps may vary slightly from those described in this project. Refer to Basic Techniques (page 6) for instruction on all the different methods.

1. Decide on your design. Minki fussy cut some little characters from a favorite fabric line and other scraps for windows and attached them with fusible web (see Creating Fabric Accents, page 14). Use this layout or create your own arrangement. As a final detail, Minki wrote her children's names above the doors.

2. Thread your sewing machine with dark thread. Set the stitch length to 1.8 and use an open-toe appliqué foot if you have one. Outline each design once or twice, depending on the level of contrast you desire.

PUT IN THE ZIPPER

1. Pin (or use Wonder Tape) the zipper in place on the raw edge of the cotton print pouch top, right sides together, aligning the top edge of the zipper with the top edge of the fabric.

2. Sew along the length of the zipper, using a zipper foot. When the zipper pull gets in your way, unzip the zipper halfway to get it out of the way.

3. Repeat Steps 1 and 2 on the other side of the outer bag to create a tube with the right side of the bag on the inside.

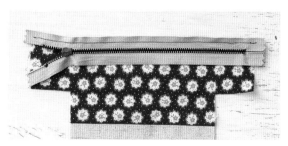

SEW THE SIDES

1. Fold the outer pouch through the linen body so the raw edges of the zippered top meet the raw edges of the linen as shown. Pin with right sides together. Fold the 2½˝-long piece of ribbon in half and insert the folded edge between the 2 pieces of fabric, centered over the zipper, to make a tab. Pin in place and sew along the 4˝ edge.

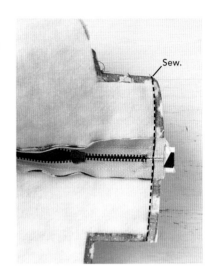

Sew.

2. Repeat Step 1 on the opposite side.

3. Your project now has 4 openings that will be sewn up to create the sides. Starting on any side, pinch the ends of an opening together to flatten the material. Match up the seams where the linen meets the cotton print and pin well. Sew together along this edge. Make sure to backstitch at the beginning and end of the seam for strength. Repeat on the 3 remaining sides.

TIP *To make installing the zipper a little bit easier, handstitch the zipper ends closed before you install it.*

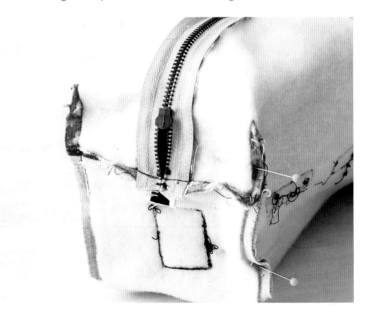

MAKE THE LINING

1. Fuse the lining interfacing to the wrong side of the lining fabric.

2. Press each long end of the lining fabric ¼˝ toward the wrong side. Place the lining piece right side up. With right sides together, match the corners of the 2 ends to the corners of the side tabs. Pin and sew, making sure to backstitch at the beginning and end of the seam. Repeat on the opposite side.

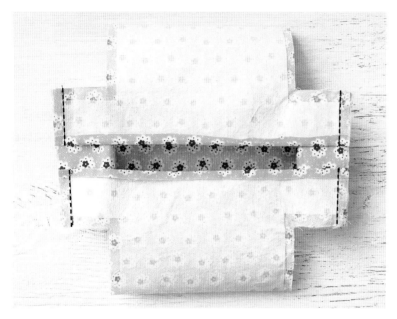

3. Sew up the lining sides in the same manner as the outer pouch sides.

FINISH IT UP

Turn the lining right side out. Slip the outside pouch into the lining, wrong sides together. Pin the lining to the zipper, folding the raw edge to the inside, and hand stitch in place. Turn the pouch right side out.

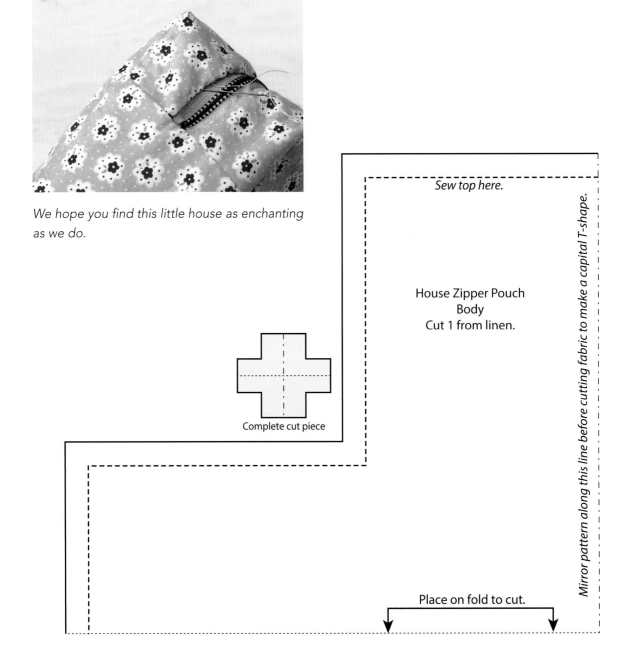

We hope you find this little house as enchanting as we do.

Complete cut piece

Sew top here.

House Zipper Pouch
Body
Cut 1 from linen.

Mirror pattern along this line before cutting fabric to make a capital T-shape.

Place on fold to cut.

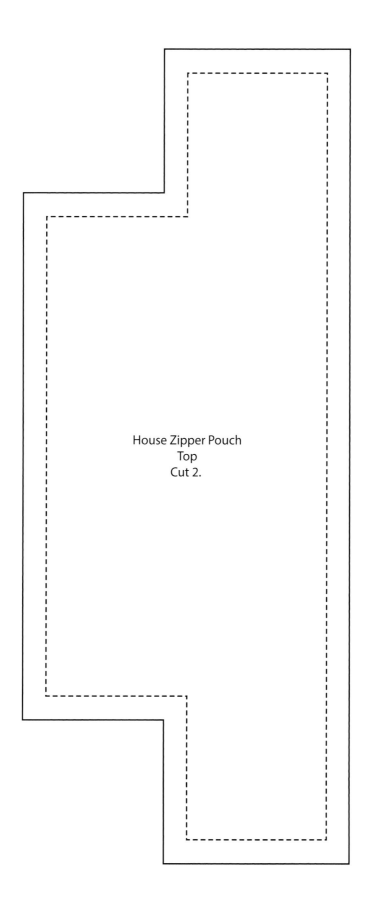

House Zipper Pouch
Top
Cut 2.

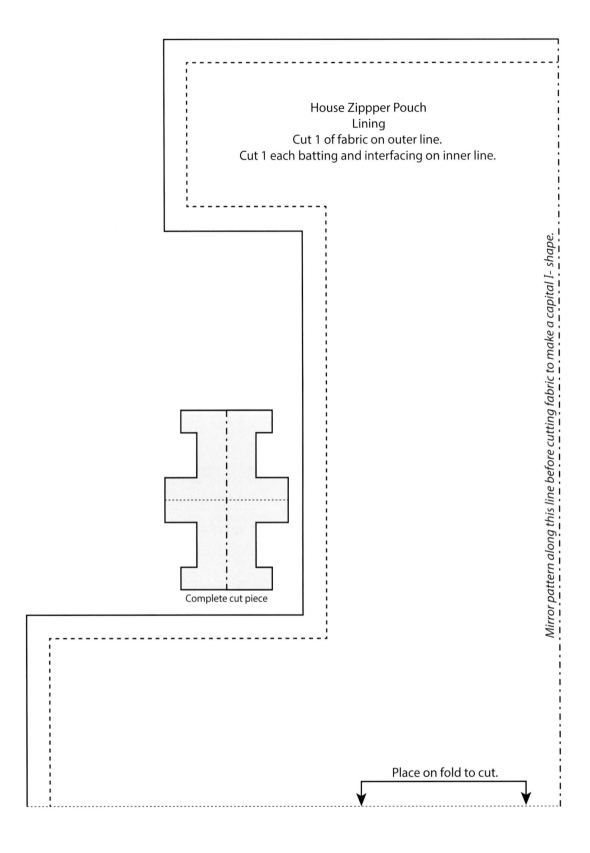

House Zippper Pouch
Lining
Cut 1 of fabric on outer line.
Cut 1 each batting and interfacing on inner line.

Complete cut piece

Mirror pattern along this line before cutting fabric to make a capital I- shape.

Place on fold to cut.

Let your dreams fly high

Photo by Minki Kim

WORDS TO LIVE BY CUSHION

Designed and made by Minki Kim | Finished size: 14˝ × 14˝

One of the greatest joys of sewing is creating things for the people you love. It is very satisfying to create something that you know each person will enjoy. When the preteens in your life outgrow dolls and doll clothes, stitch up these cushions for their bedrooms to remind them to dream big every day, or use a message that is close to your heart that you will enjoy seeing every day.

NEUTRAL COTTON FOR FRONT:
1 fat quarter

COTTON PRINT FOR BACK:
⅜ yard

COTTON SCRAPS FOR FABRIC ACCENTS: Various colors and sizes

PILLOW FORM: 14″ × 14″

PAPER-BACKED FUSIBLE WEB: such as Steam-A-Seam

WASH-AWAY STABILIZER (SUCH AS WASH-AWAY STITCH STABILIZER, BY C&T PUBLISHING): 1 sheet

EMBROIDERY BACKING PAPER OR STABILIZER: Small scrap

FABRIC MARKER: Frixion pen or water-soluble marker

MACHINE SEWING THREAD: Neutral for piecing and dark 40-weight and a complementary color in 12-weight for a bold outline (Minki used black and blue here.)

CUTTING

NEUTRAL COTTON FOR FRONT:
1 piece 14½″ × 14½″

COTTON PRINT FOR BACK:
2 pieces 10″ × 14½″

EMBROIDERY BACKING PAPER OR STABILIZER: 1 piece 4″ × 6″

INSTRUCTIONS

Seam allowances are ¼″ unless otherwise noted.

PREPARE THE DESIGN

Transfer technique shown: Fusible web for the air balloon and clouds, and wash-away stabilizer for the words. Print or trace the patterns onto the fusible web (remember to reverse the designs) and/or wash-away stabilizer.

If you choose different techniques for transferring and appliqué than those used here, the materials and steps may vary slightly from those described in this project. Refer to Basic Techniques (page 6) for instruction on all the different methods.

1. Transfer the Words to Live By designs (pages 101 and 102) using your method of choice (see Transferring a Design to Fabric, page 6, and Creating Fabric Accents, page 14).

2. Cut out each section of the balloon on the fusible web, stick it to a fabric scrap, and trim the fabric. Arrange the pieces on the background fabric and fuse. Repeat with the clouds. Using a temporary marking pen, sketch in the ropes that connect the balloon to the basket.

3. Transfer the words "Let your dreams fly high" onto the background fabric.

SEWING ILLUSTRATION

1. Thread your sewing machine with dark thread. Set the stitch length to 2.0–2.5 and use an open-toe appliqué foot if you have one. Stitch around each fabric accent, very close to the edge. Stitch in the rope detail.

2. Place embroidery backing paper or stabilizer under the words.

3. Thread your sewing machine with 12-weight thread for this part of the design, for a bold line. Outline the writing. Remove any excess embroidery backing paper or stabilizer.

4. If you used wash-away stabilizer, rinse under cool running water to dissolve it. Set aside to dry or iron to dry the fabric more quickly.

MAKE THE PILLOW BACK

On the 2 pillow back pieces, fold a 14½˝ edge over ¼˝ to the wrong side and press. Fold ¼˝ again and press. Topstitch about ⅛˝ from the edge.

PUT IT TOGETHER

1. Place the pillow front right side up on your work surface. Place a pillow back piece on top of it, right sides together, aligning the raw edges along the top. Place the second pillow back piece on top of that, aligning the raw edges along the bottom. Sew around the outside edge, reinforcing the overlapping section several times. Clip the corners.

2. To prevent fraying when you wash the pillow cover, zigzag stitch around the raw edges of the pillow cover or use a serger if you have one.

FINISH IT UP

1. Turn the pillow right side out and press.

2. Insert a 14˝ × 14˝ pillow form.

Stitch up a few more of these pillows with different inspiring messages.

Let your dreams Fly high

Words to Live By design
(For iron-on transfer, see pullout page P1.)

Words to Live By fabric accents
(For iron-on transfer, see pullout page P1.)

HOOP ART

Designed and made by Minki Kim | Finished size: 10˝ × 10˝

We love to be surrounded by meaningful art in our homes, such as little scenes that make us happy. This project provides an example of something you can stitch up and display where you can see it every day. This little scene touches on several themes that we hope will bring a smile to your face—rain boots, teacups, teapots, and picnic baskets, to name just a few.

MATERIALS AND SUPPLIES

LINEN: Large scrap
(see Cutting for size)

COTTON SCRAPS:
Various colors and sizes

**WASH-AWAY STABILIZER, SUCH AS
WASH-AWAY STITCH STABILIZER
(BY C&T PUBLISHING):** 1 sheet

**FUSIBLE MIDWEIGHT INTERFACING
(SUCH AS PELLON 931TD):**
20˝ wide, large scrap
(see Cutting for size)

WOODEN EMBROIDERY HOOP:
10˝ diameter

FABRIC MARKER: Frixion pen
or water-soluble marker

MACHINE SEWING THREAD:
Neutral (white or ivory)
for piecing and dark
40-weight for outlining

HAND-SEWING NEEDLES:
Regular

FABRIC GLUE STICK

CUTTING

LINEN: 1 piece 14˝ × 14˝

FUSIBLE MIDWEIGHT INTERFACING:
1 piece 8½˝ × 11˝

INSTRUCTIONS

Seam allowances are ¼˝ unless otherwise noted.

PREPARE THE DESIGN

Transfer technique shown: Wash-away stabilizer.

If you choose a different technique than the one used here, the materials and steps may vary slightly from those described in this project. Refer to Basic Techniques (page 6) for instruction on all the different methods.

1. Fuse the interfacing to the wrong side of the linen, in the area where the design will be.

2. Copy or trace the Hoop Art design (page 107) using your method of choice (see Creating Fabric Accents, page 14). If you are using wash-away stabilizer, don't attach the stabilizer to the background fabric yet.

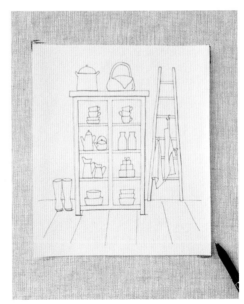

TIP *Create artwork meaningful to you by sketching out your own design or tracing your child's drawing. Then use this technique to create a family treasure!*

----

3. Mark each corner of the stabilizer on the right side of the linen with a temporary marking pen.

4. Cut out the items on each of the shelves from wash-away stabilizer, keeping the shelf and ladder intact. Next, remove the backing and stick the small items to the fabric scraps of your choice. Trim away excess fabric.

5. After the shelf and ladder items are cut out, remove the backing and stick the remaining portion of the illustration, centered, onto the right side of the linen. Arrange the fabric accents on each of the shelves and glue them in place. Sketch in any additional details, such as handles, bows, and the lines on the floor.

1. Thread your sewing machine with neutral thread. Set the stitch length to 1.4 and use an open-toe appliqué foot if you have one.

2. Secure the fabric accents to the background by stitching about ⅛″ inside the edge of each piece with neutral thread.

3. Thread your sewing machine with dark thread. Stitch around each fabric accent, very close to the edge. Outline each piece once or twice, depending on the line thickness you desire. Lastly, stitch any details such as cup handles, ribbons, and the lines on the floor.

4. If you are using wash-away stabilizer, rinse the piece under cool running water to dissolve the stabilizer. Set it aside to dry.

FRAME IT

1. Press the artwork and place the hoop over it for placement. Draw a circle 2½″ bigger than the hoop. Trim away the excess linen.

TIP *When you iron, make sure to cover the design with a press cloth, so that any remaining stabilizer residue doesn't stick to your iron.*

2. To prevent the edges of the linen from fraying, sew a zigzag stitch around the edge of the linen, or use a serger if you have one.

3. Place the artwork inside the hoop. Thread a needle with a long piece of thread and sew a running stitch about ¾″ from the edge of the fabric. Pull the thread gently to gather the edges on the back of the hoop. Backstitch a couple of times to secure the stiches and knot the thread to secure.

Hang your lovely personal artwork in a place where it will bring you joy every day.

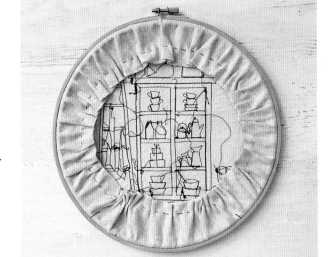

Hoop Art design
(For iron-on transfer, see pullout page P2.)

VIGNETTE

Designed and made by Minki Kim | Finished size: 14˝ × 11˝

Isn't it fun to create little vignettes of everyday items arranged just so? There is so much joy to be found in the simple pleasures of a beloved sewing machine, a cup of tea, and a scattering of sewing notions. Capture them with sewing illustration, to be visited again and again.

LINEN: 1 large scrap
or fat quarter

COTTON SCRAPS:
Various colors and sizes

**WASH-AWAY STABILIZER (SUCH AS
WASH-AWAY STITCH STABILIZER,
BY C&T PUBLISHING):** 1 sheet

**PAPER-BACKED FUSIBLE WEB
(SUCH AS STEAM-A-STEAM):**
1 piece 8½˝ × 11˝

**FUSIBLE MIDWEIGHT INTERFACING
(SUCH AS PELLON 931TD):**
1 piece 8½˝ × 11˝

FABRIC MARKER: Frixion pen
or water-soluble marker

SEWING MACHINE THREAD:
Neutral (white or ivory)
for piecing and dark
40-weight for outlining

FABRIC GLUE STICK

FRAME:
11˝ × 14˝ for the project
as shown

CUTTING

LINEN: 1 piece 19˝ × 18˝
(or however large you
need it to fit your frame)

PAPER-BACKED FUSIBLE WEB:
1 piece 8½˝ × 11˝

FUSIBLE MIDWEIGHT INTERFACING:
1 piece 8½˝ × 11˝

INSTRUCTIONS

Seam allowances are ¼˝ unless otherwise noted.

PREPARE THE DESIGN

*Transfer technique shown: Fusible web for the sewing machine
(photocopy or trace), wash-away stabilizer for the rest of the
pattern.*

*If you choose different techniques for transferring and appliqué
than those used here, the materials and steps may vary slightly
from those described in this project. Refer to Basic Techniques
(page 6) for instruction on all the different methods.*

1. Fuse the interfacing to the wrong side of the linen, in the area
where the design will be.

2. Transfer the entire Vignette design (page 112) to a sheet of
wash-away stabilizer (see Creating Fabric Accents, page 14).
Transfer the sewing machine portion of the design to a print
fabric scrap, using your method of choice. *Note: Fusible web
works best for large design elements such as the sewing
machine because of the way it secures the larger pieces of
fabric to the linen.*

TIP *Feel free to draw or trace your own scene to create a
one-of-a-kind artwork that is uniquely yours.*

----

3. Fuse the sewing machine image to the linen.

4. Place the wash-away stabilizer with the entire design on top of the linen. Mark each corner of the sheet of stabilizer onto the linen with a temporary marking pen for reference. One at a time, carefully cut out each design element that will be a fabric accent. Stick that 1 element on the fabric of your choice and trim carefully; then glue it in place on the linen background.

5. Continue in the same fashion with all the fabric accents, carefully cutting out each element, adhering it to the fabric scraps, and gluing it in place. Take your time and enjoy the process!

TIP *Projects such as this are a great way to use up all those precious fabric scraps that you just can't bear to throw away.*

6. When your design is arranged, sketch in any additional details.

SEWING ILLUSTRATION

1. Thread your sewing machine with neutral thread. Set the stitch length to 1.6 or 1.8 and use an open-toe appliqué foot if you have one.

2. Secure the fabric accents to the background by stitching about ⅛″ inside the edge of each piece with neutral thread. *Note: Securing the fabric accents is not necessary if you used fusible web.*

3. Thread your sewing machine with dark thread. Stitch around each fabric accent very close to the edge. Outline each piece once or twice, depending on the line thickness you prefer. Lastly, stitch any details such as the word on the cup, details of the sewing machine, and other thread-only parts of the design.

4. Rinse under cool running water to dissolve the wash-away stabilizer. Set aside to dry. Press from the wrong side.

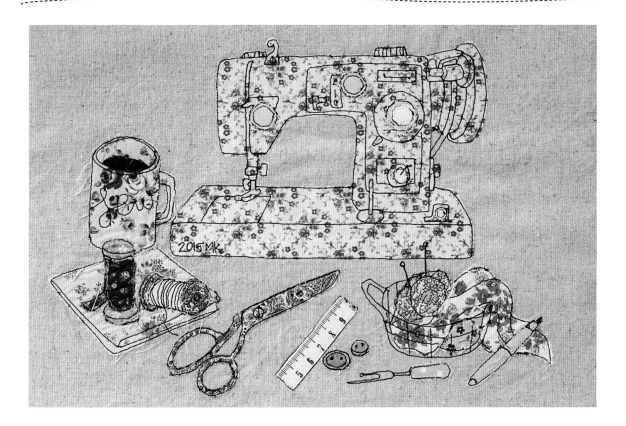

FRAME IT

There are many ways to display this type of artwork. Standard picture frames, shadow boxes, and stretching the linen over canvas all create lovely pieces of art for your home. Tape, zigzag stitch, or serge the raw edges of the linen to prevent it from fraying. Use fabric-safe adhesive spray on the backing to secure it smoothly, or just wrap the linen around the backing and tape or staple it from the back.

We hope you will find joy in the simple pleasures of everyday life each time you look at this project.

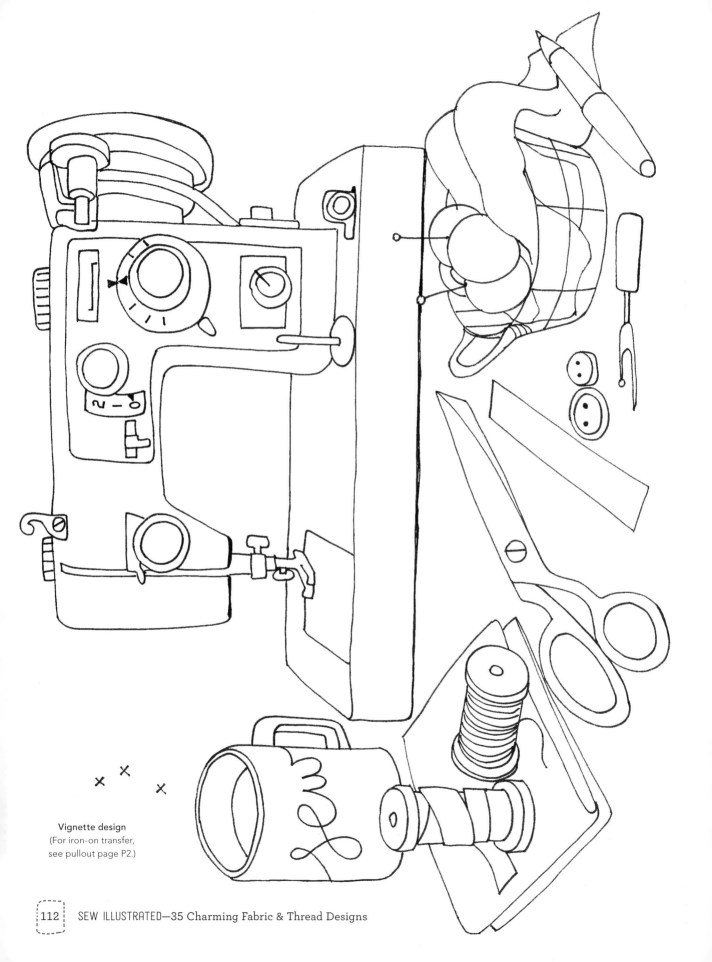

Vignette design
(For iron-on transfer,
see pullout page P2.)

FAMILY PICTURE

Designed and made by Minki Kim | Finished size: 11˝ × 14˝

Childhood is so fleeting; capture as many precious but everyday moments of it as you can. This piece of art began as a photo that Minki snapped with her phone on the way to the park one evening. By transforming moments such as these into artwork, you can remember them as if they happened yesterday.

LINEN: 1 large scrap or fat quarter or the size that fits your frame

COTTON SCRAPS: Various colors and sizes

WASH-AWAY STABILIZER (SUCH AS WASH-AWAY STITCH STABILIZER, BY C&T PUBLISHING): 1 sheet

FUSIBLE MIDWEIGHT INTERFACING (SUCH AS PELLON 31TD): 1 large scrap

FABRIC MARKER: Frixion pen or water-soluble marker

SEWING MACHINE THREAD: Neutral (white or ivory) for appliqué and dark 40-weight for outlining

FABRIC GLUE STICK

FRAME: 11″ × 14″ for project as shown (optional)

CUTTING

LINEN: 1 piece 12″ × 15″ or the size that fits your frame

FUSIBLE MIDWEIGHT INTERFACING: 1 piece 8½″ × 11″

INSTRUCTIONS

PREPARE THE DESIGN

Seam allowances are ¼″ unless otherwise noted.

Transfer technique shown: Wash-away stabilizer.

If you choose different techniques for transferring and appliqué than those used here, the materials and steps may vary slightly from those described in this project. Refer to Basic Techniques (page 6) for instruction on all the different methods.

1. Fuse the interfacing to the wrong side of the linen, in the area where the design will be.

2. Transfer the Family Picture design (page 117) or create your own using your method of choice (see Creating Fabric Accents, page 14).

TIP *Another option is to print a photo right onto the wash-away stabilizer and then outline and fill it in with dark thread. The result will be like a black-and-white sketch.*

3. Place the wash-away stabilizer with the entire design on top of the linen. Mark the corners of the sheet of stabilizer on the linen with a temporary marking pen for alignment reference. One at a time, carefully cut out each area that will be a fabric accent. Remove the backing and stick that 1 element on the fabric of your choice and trim carefully. Glue it in place on the linen background.

4. Continue in the same fashion with all the fabric accents, carefully cutting out each element, adhering it to a fabric scrap, and gluing it in place. Take your time and enjoy the process! In areas where the elements overlap, cut the bottom piece a little larger so that the top piece will overlap it completely.

TIP *Try using your children's old clothes for the fabric accents whenever possible. That way it's doubly special!*

SEWING ILLUSTRATION

1. Thread your sewing machine with neutral (white or ivory) thread. Set the stitch length to anywhere from 1.2 to 1.6, depending on the level of detail in the design, and use an open-toe appliqué foot if you have one. Secure the fabric accents to the background by stitching about ⅛″ inside the edge of each piece.

2. Thread your sewing machine with dark thread. Stitch around each fabric accent, very close to the edge. Outline each piece once or twice, depending on the level of contrast you desire. Lastly, stitch any details like faces, hands, and clothing details.

3. Rinse under cool running water to dissolve the wash-away stabilizer. Set aside to dry. Press from the wrong side. After you have washed away the stabilizer, take another look at the design to see if you missed any elements or want to add any finishing touches.

FRAME IT

There are many ways to display this type of artwork. Standard picture frames, shadow boxes, and stretching the linen over canvas all create lovely pieces of art for your home. Tape, zigzag stitch, or serge the raw edges of the linen to prevent it from fraying. Use fabric-safe adhesive spray on the backing to secure it smoothly, or just wrap the linen around the backing and tape or staple it from the back.

Enjoy being reminded of your lovely family each time you pass this special piece of handiwork.

About the Authors

Kristin Esser and Minki Kim

MINKI KIM is a formally trained artist and self-taught sewist. She discovered sewing as a creative outlet when her children were small and she wanted to capture the beauty of ordinary moments, first with hand embroidery and later recreating them with her sewing machine and fabric—literally drawing with thread. Originally from Korea, Minki now calls Southern California home, where she lives with her husband and three young daughters. On any given day you can find her in her sewing room creating projects to share on her blog, minkikim.com, in her pattern shop, sewingillustration.com, and on Instagram.

KRISTIN ESSER has been surrounded by sewing and crafting since childhood. She dabbled in apparel sewing but eventually found her passion in quilting, craft sewing, and knitting. She lives just down the street from Minki, where she has written Minki's patterns and tutorials for publication in industry magazines. She writes about her creative pursuits and her life with her husband and three teenage children at kristinesser.com.

Resources

Some of the listed resources are wholesale only and do not sell to individual consumers. They are listed because the websites provide information, including where to purchase the products.

FABRIC

There are many great sources for fabric; these are a few favorites, especially for 1930s reproductions.

- Moda Fabrics—modafabrics.com
- Penny Rose Fabrics—pennyrosefabrics.com
- Riley Blake Designs—rileyblakedesigns.com

LINEN

Linen can be hard to find; here are some good sources.

- Gray Line Linen—graylinelinen.com (We used the "Barry" and "Judy" linens in a variety of natural shades.)
- Jo-Ann Fabric and Craft Stores—joann.com
- Moda Fabrics—modafabrics.com

ONLINE SHOPS

- Fat Quarter Shop—fatquartershop.com
- Sew Me A Song— etsy.com/shop/sewmeasong
- Vintage Notion—etsy.com/shop/jhwa

NOTIONS

Thread and embroidery floss

- Aurifil—aurifil.com
- DMC—dmc-usa.com

Buttons

- Buttons.com—buttons.com
- Jillibean Soup—jillibean-soup.com
- Just Another Button Co.— justanotherbuttoncompany.com

Batting, fusible web, interfacing, wash-away stabilizer

- C&T Publishing—ctpub.com
- The Warm Co.—warmcompany.com

Trims

- Billy Cotton Shop— etsy.com/shop/billycottonshop0413
- Simplicity—simplicity.com

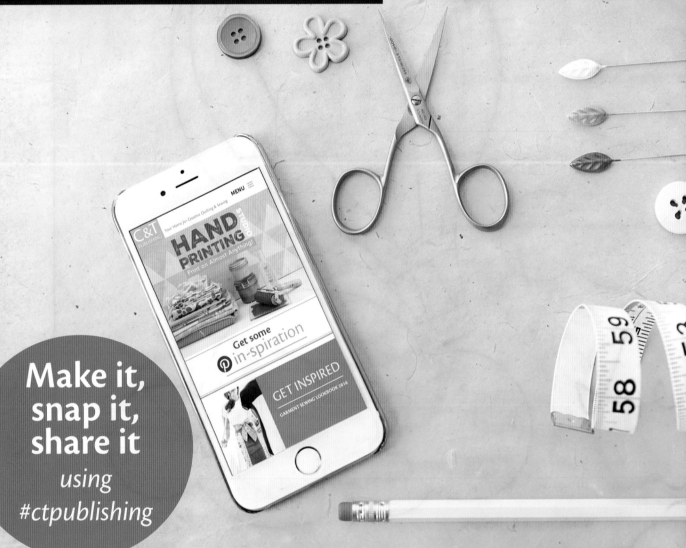